Books by Cynthia Macdonald

LIVING WILLS: NEW AND SELECTED POEMS   1991

ALTERNATE MEANS OF TRANSPORT   1985

(W)HOLES   1980

TRANSPLANTS   1976

AMPUTATIONS   1972

LIVING WILLS: NEW AND SELECTED POEMS

CYNTHIA MACDONALD

LIVING WILLS

New & Selected Poems

*Insribed for June-Simbling
in Austin, October, 1992*

Cynthia M

 Alfred A. Knopf   New York   1991

Poems from the following previously published books are included in this volume:

AMPUTATIONS, copyright © 1972 by Cynthia Macdonald; originally published by
George Braziller, Inc. *The New American Review*: "Instruction from Bly" from
Amputations.

TRANSPLANTS, copyright © 1976 by Cynthia Macdonald; originally published by
George Braziller, Inc.

(w)HOLES, copyright © 1977, 1978, 1979, 1980 by Cynthia Macdonald;
originally published by Alfred A. Knopf, Inc.

ALTERNATE MEANS OF TRANSPORT, copyright © 1980, 1981, 1982, 1983, 1985
by Cynthia Macdonald; originally published by Alfred A. Knopf, Inc.
"Apartments on First Avenue" from *Alternate Means of Transport* was originally
published in *New York: Poems*, edited by Howard Moss, published by Avon Books
in 1980.

Acknowledgment is made to the following publications in which the new poems in this
book first appeared: *Antaeus*: "The Precise Shape of a Wave"; *The New Republic*: "A Past
Due Notice" and "A Critical Age"; *The Yale Review*: "Separations" and "The Murderer's
Daughter"; *Parnassus: Poetry in Review*: "Envy of Old Husbands" and "Prayer for the De-
serving"; *The New Yorker*: "The Triborough Bridge A Crown for His Head."

The sequence "At the Round Earth's Imagin'd Corners" was written in conjunction with
the artist, James Surls, for a show of collaborations between artists and writers, entitled
One + One. Our piece was later purchased by The Museum of Fine Arts, Houston.

The title, *Living Wills*, was the creation of artists, Hillary Leone and Jennifer Macdonald,
who lovingly willed it to me.

The generosity of The John Simon Guggenheim Foundation gave me needed time in which
to write much of the new work in this book. The MacDowell Colony gave me necessary
silence.

Thanks to my friends Jane Cooper and Edward Hirsch for their help.

Library of Congress Cataloging-in-Publication Data

MacDonald, Cynthia.
    Living wills : new and selected poems / by Cynthia Macdonald. —
1st ed.—
      p. cm.
      ISBN 0–394–58503–8
      I. Title.
PS3563.A276L58   1991   90–52737
811'.54—dc20   CIP

FOR JENNIFER TIM MACDONALD
AND FOR SCOTT THURSTON MACDONALD

Poems published in earlier volumes are indicated as follows:
* AMPUTATIONS
† TRANSPLANTS
‡ (W)HOLES
§ ALTERNATE MEANS OF TRANSPORT

I THE PRECISE SHAPE OF A WAVE

THE PRECISE SHAPE OF A WAVE

Hokusai lived in ninety-six houses.
Do you believe that? Probably. Print is
Certainty's fixative. Actually, he lived in ninety-three.
I believe that because someone who ought to know
Told me. Hokusai may have miscounted, occupied
With the precise shape of a wave, and its relation to
The arched back of his spotted cat, the kind we call
Calico, but they call flecked, spotted with water drops.
Do you believe they call it flecked? Look at his design
For Printed Luxury Envelopes: "Cat Trying to Fish
    The Moon out of the Water to See the Truth."
No, that was Hiroshige, and it was a monkey.
Hiroshige, Hokusai. Edo's twins. One of them wore
    A hat of snow, the way the houses did
On the Tokaido road in winter. The snow hat
Kept his head from burning up. Hokusai lived
Till ninety: *Is a cool head the artist's fixative?*

Perhaps the prefecture in which he lived
    Had records of each person in each house
    So it is possible to tally the exact number.
*Do you believe Harold Bloom when he claims
Whitman intended* "tally" *in* "To the tally of my soul,
    Loud and strong kept up the grey brown bird,"
To refer to Whitman's/Lincoln's privates? Genital or
    Military. Is there a distinction? A whole theory
Blooms amid the lilacs from "the tally." Unfortunately,
    Such seminal theories stick to the poem
No matter how we try to wash them off. To tally is
Important in Japan: babies chew the hard beads of

The abacus while teething. The koban in each district
　　Keeps precise lists of who lives where, but
　Perhaps Saito-San near Ueno Park, wishing good luck
　To the debtors walking by his *koban* to spend the night
　Under the unpetalled trees, drank too much and forgot
　　To enter seven new arrivals in the New Year's lists.
　　Perhaps Hokusai was one of them. *How many times*
　Do you believe Hokusai changed his name? He was called
Katsukawa Shunro, Tamekazu, Shoshunro and Gumbatei Gyobatsu.
　But was that all? How many times did he change his face?

　　Your Uncle Morgan's wife told me he made her shave
　　Her pubic hair. If you told him that you knew, would he
　　　Change his name and face and move to Cleveland?
　　Do you believe me that he made her shave her muff?
　　You think he's wise, pulling on his beard, lecturing on
Puts and takes. Belief is based on the source: Morgan Guaranty
　　　Shifts only when there is a run on the bank;
　　　Then the river slips and slides and overflows
　Like a kimono wrapping a naked body and trailing after.
　　No doubt you don't believe it—so Midwestern,
　　Turning your head away, never licking the night.
　　Do you believe that André is the one who told me,
　As we lay on the peach silk futon after we had articulated
The precise shape of a wave, how many houses Hokusai lived in?

A PAST-DUE NOTICE

It isn't what you think; it's what you say
You see—they were . . . not hidden by the sea . . .
You never should have spoken your dismay

And yet you did, beside Great Heron Bay,
Though with such pinched, such dry formality . . .
It isn't what you think, it's what you say,

"I saw the two of you out on the quay."
He smiled his perfect smile, "not quay; it's key."
He never seemed to notice my dismay.

I spoke again. He turned and walked away
As he so often had; he'd seldom disagree.
It isn't what you think; it's what you say

And what you don't; we both avoid the fray.
The herons mimicked our civility.
They never seemed to notice our dismay.

Ulysses won't return—no passion play
For us, but then I'm not Penelope:
The wine-dark sea I see as dark red ink.
It isn't what you say; it's what you think.

VAIN REMEDY

How deep and urgent the need for more is,
The need to fill and nourish,
The need to be filled, to be nourished.
Granny said *The Ladies' Gazette* and *Modern Maid* were full
Of advertisements for weight loss. Yes, even in those days
Of caressed rotundity, of face-cheeks like peaches
And bottom-cheeks like long-grown honeydews,
Reducing remedies crowded the back pages:
A Waist to Fit in the Ring of His Hands, A Swan Neck
Like Anna Pavlova's, who must have shunned the confection
Of cream and jam and cake named in her honor.

And thin they got and thin and thinner
Until they lay on beds or divans like blue gauze veils.
They ate their fill, *Mutton Marinated in Red Wine,*
Farina Pudding, Fruits of the Sea Gratiné
And more, and were not nourished, like lovers
Who have a need to fill and to be filled which
Never is fulfilled. A husband's thumb
And forefinger could circle their waists:
They wasted away before his very eyes because
The pills they swallowed were sugar shells
Around tape worms,
Granny told me; it was true.
And so they ate and ate and failed, faded
Like the rosy bud, worm coiled within.

This is the stuff which cannot yield contentment,
This is the suck on a breast full of water. This is
The mirror's kiss. These are the sweet exchanges
Which are not flesh, kisses which kiss the air.
This is longing: the worm boring toward the heart,
Lengthening itself through an intricate life.

It is as if I have a fever,
As if I were little Cynny
Standing in the doorway,
Framed, a pretty picture, waving bye-bye
To them, who were off again,
Going out again, or away again.
My arms are hot and hurt
As if the fever is spreading the way it did
Through her, my sister Ginny, right up
Into her ear as if a yellow jacket got in there
And buzzed until she couldn't hear,
And flew from her ear to her nose
Stuffing it with the yellow powder of its feet,
And walked to her eyes and stung them dead,
And she must have cried
Because she died of *mastoids*.
That is what Granny said she died of
When she said you must never mention her name to
Them because they are very sad
Losing a child that way.
And they went out, and they went away
To have a good time,
And I stood on the steps waving,
And they lost me
As if I were the diamond earring
Mummy couldn't find after the Feiner's party,
And she had only one left
Like a star, up so high, in the sky
Where—but little Cynny never did say her name—she was.

Older, nickname gone, parents gone,
I stand in the doorway, smiling:
There is no way to hold on or
There will be nothing to hold on to.
So the fever climbs my arms
As if it were the black widow Daddy warned me about
But I have to say,
"Goodbye, have a good trip." As if I were the widow,
Black and desolate, ready
To slice the black sky into widow's ribbons
Using the diamond's cutting edge
Because I am so sad,
Because I cannot help it.

THE MURDERER'S DAUGHTER:
INSIDE AND OUTSIDE

One down, one to go. Could her father have said that? Could her father
Have meant her? Her father who would never let her sit on his lap.
Farther into the reel, his voice hoarse: *One to go.* Take out food:
His favorite peanut butter sandwich, chocolate shake. His voice shook.
Grief or anger. They said he was undone when Virginia died. My sister,
Virginia, intact, of course, at six, that small Jewish girl enacting
Her name. White and quiet. Undone. They said he was undone.
Yet her mother told her he did not like children, did not want
Any more. *Cut.* His murders then, blood dripping drop by drop
Like a leaking faucet, were only in the movies he wrote:
Franchot Tone, wearing gloves, crept in the bright Hollywood dark
Toward the window, his eyes flinty. *Cut.* The film, not the throat; that
Came later. The remaining daughter watched without a sense of peril.
Franchot Tone crept again and again in the bright Hollywood dark,
Toward the window, whispering to the mike. "Two down, two to go."
Cut. Her father's eyes turned on her were blank screens or, filled
With anger, steel doors on vaults. He never stole doors, he stole love.
He huddled with it, kept it to himself like a child with a blanket.

Could he have said it, wearing his steel-blue stolen eyes, *One down,*
One to go ... Cut. Another shake. Take out food.
Knock it out, the way Bogart did when he pulled the Mauser
Out of his pocket; rub it out, like writers with an artgum eraser.
Delicious to eat—I nibbled his when he wasn't there: maple sugar.
His script, erased by him, smudged and erased, erased again
By the producer who gave it to somebody else in the string of writers
Kept by MGM in 1938. He sat in his wing chair, sleeping.
My mother said, "You're sleeping, Leonard, not working."

"I am not sleeping. I'm thinking." He mourned Virginia even though
Their mother said he didn't—Virginia snatched from him by scarlet
Fever—would have invoked the Lindbergh law to put the kidnapper in
The electric chair if he had had his way. But death can never be convicted.

Anger is not murder. If only I had known that. That anger is not murder.
The one remaining daughter. *One to go. Two to go.* They went.
Mother and daughter, back to New York. We went back East.
Her father wrote he was eating most of his meals in drive-ins. Until
He got another wife who got her tubes tied but TV took over anyway.
Though movies died, they were happy. I could have seen that
If I had seen them. But California was too far away.
Farther into the reel. I put on white gloves; she dusts
Important monuments with them. Bronze, dressed in its
Patinas, marble, veined and seductive, and scratchy stone.
Always in touch with memorials. *Cut.* He was the one to go. Murder.
He murdered himself. Instead of his voice when I called to stop him,
Someone with a drawl . . . "Laporte, L.A. Police Department."

Now through a window in Santa Monica I look at the surf
Flinging its boa of white feathers over and over onto the satin sea.
The window is at right angles to the shore, although the view
Is seen, then reconstructed like memory, as if it were without
Impediment. Here, where I am closer to him, I polish the window
With my white gloves. You would hardly know there is anything
Between me and the sharp sea air and the stolen eyes. But she,
Shining the pane, she, removing every smudge, sees against
The sea's glass screen a reflection of the slow, soft murderer.

ENVY OF OLD HUSBANDS

Starting over. Like water gone
Cold. Turn to off;
Wait five minutes; push the red
Button until flame ignites.
Is there a touch of blue in it, or is that
A memory of old gas stoves
Where the blue came from something the Gas Co.
Put in to warn us of dangers?
Warming. A ring of dancing flames.
The silken richness of young wives
Fit for a Sultan, meet for a King, appropriate
For middle age when men start over.
And they pick well: beauties, kind, able to
Discuss K'ang-hsi or Kant insightfully,
Incisively. Able to give old husbands
Babies. But old husbands do not want babies. Theirs
Are grown. Young wives do and what is meet is met.

I watch with envy, not wishing to be the young wife
With all the truths and loves of motherhood—
I've had them—but to be the old father
Whose years can be redeemed, like bonds
Which mature in a safe deposit box, as easily as
Opening a lovely green cabbage and finding—
O, yes, I do wish it—an even lovelier baby
With nurse and lover attached like a gift card.

A CERTAIN DISTINCTION

These men are gentlemanly.
They are almost all tall.
It is more difficult to move
With courtly solicitude if you
Are short. A few are, but then
They are thin. They are all
Thin, including those who are tall.

They are famous. And over
Fifty. Younger men do not
Know how to do it. They never
Learned, which is blamed
On Freud and John Dewey.
That may be partly true,
But it is like saying if you put
Sea water in the espresso pot,
The coffee is too salty.

The men are taking their kids
To the park or the planetarium
Or the hardware store on Saturday.
A few of them know how to fix
Faulty devices; most do not, but
They deal with what they cannot do
As if the distinction between
The real and imagined could be seen
As a matter of equilibrium.

They lean over to kiss a daughter's
Hand or tie a son's shoe uncertain
About what causes the pain in their hearts.
Thin men, famous, humming an etude,
Striking a grace note, bending:
Passion concealed as solicitude.

THE SOUNDING CATARACT

1) a waterfall, properly one of considerable size, falling headlong over a precipice; 2) an opacity of the crystalline lens of the eye.

This is a cat. And this is a cataract.
Water falls into the pool of nine lives,
Licking itself as it curls into lazy rounds.
On just such distinctions—cat and cataract—
Lives may depend, hang like a silk and gold
Fringe. The cat, contented after a day
Of creamy satisfactions, scents the ineffable
And whips its body toward it, only to find
It was not dreaming on the quilted window
Ledge, but beside the engorged cataract,
That it, mid-air, cannot change course.
Its eyes, grasping the watery descent,
The rocks and rills in their white lace cuffs,
Reel the final seconds in as it reels toward
The rock bed which receives the body hardly,
And it lies broken, eyes filming over,
Catapulted out of its life into
Perhaps a tenth. Or perhaps
The cat lies inert, curled in the pool of
Its mother, licked clean by
The play of her soft, rough tongue.

This is a cat. And this is a cataract
Whose water veils the end of the story
Because there is blindness necessary for survival:
A mother who turned her face away as her husband,
The father, stroked his daughter's pussy, moaning,

Listens, years later, after the mother had done what she could—
Not enough, nothing will ever be enough—for the daughter
Has only one life and it cannot be mended, but the mother listens
As the daughter tells how the man who lives in
The apartment below on West 30th has murdered her kitten,
How she found it floating in the sink which had been covered
With the boards those old brownstone houses have to
Make a sink a counter, and how the underside was scratched
With claw marks which the kitten made, trying to escape.
She says they said the man was in a rage because a pipe
Had burst and water pried its way through plaster
And fell on him as he lay sleeping. In the hall the neighbors
Heard the yell, "Piss, piss, she pissed on me," but no one dared
To challenge him. The woman that he lived with refused
Over and over to press charges; police were forced
To turn away although they saw the bruises and the breaks.

This is a cat and this is a cataract and this is a daughter.
I hold her close, in my arms, wanting a machine gun
As rage pours over the edge like piss onto the man
In the apartment below who is also that other man:
A flood, a cataract, the thumbprint of blindness, an indictment
Which cannot be washed away in this unintelligible world.

PRAYER FOR THE DESERVING

May you lose skin layer by layer as burn
Victims do; so you lie without protection
In the agony which liars earn.
May you swim through sleep, turn,
Remembering you cannot swim and find
The sea above you, too. Wake under water,
Choking; it will never quite kill you. Take
Care, as you must, always must before bed, to line
The items on your bureau in parade order.
May you turn, like spoiled milk, and find them
Disarrayed. May your daughter
Become the woman she could be and listen to you
As patiently and cruelly as you, in your fashion,
Heard her out, like a fishing line playing its trout
Melodies. May you love as you loved the woman in blue,
And may she love you with such passion
That you know she will never leave
Until she goes taking everything
But her felt Magritte hat. Grieve
As I grieved for you. In this time
Of your astonishment, may the mine you hid
In your closet explode. Before he cracks apart,
May your son call you what you are and find peace.
May he deny euthanasia as you turn in your restless bed
Of salt, as you lie, begging for release.
No second chance. Lie and turn,
Lie and turn in your glass bed of pain.
May you see what you have tried not to see:
You will die again and again.

May I see what I have tried not to see.
May this prayer turn out, like soldiers at
The call to arms, not to be for me.

Corpus Christi, Texas

The rabbi and his wife live in the body of Christ.
They break bread in it and drink dark, red Mogen David
To break the Yom Kippur fast. The ribs of the city
Rise around them, and its long watery arms and legs
Embrace them as the belt of the causeway lights up at dusk,
Securing the sky's dark fabric around the heart of the town,
Covering its pubis, South Bluff Park, which shelters
The strolling Rabbi and his wife from the Gulf Coast's sexual heat.
The city's beard, seaweed studded with shrimp, oysters and crayfish,
Hangs from the face of the sea with its changeable weathers—
Tense as religion or grammar, calm as beatitude or the full moon,
Joyous as a dance in the shtetl or on Fat Tuesday, as the mouth's
First savour of Aunt Martha's matzoh balls, swimming
In a richer salty broth. The eyes of Christ span the gulf of
Time looking back at himself, just after B.C., when he sat
At the long table, dividing the Passover matzoh. There was no
Poland yet so the matzoh was still a wafer, flat as the world.

The Rabbi prepares for Yom Kippur. His best friend is
The Methodist minister. Perhaps here in Corpus Christi—the body
Of Christ—there will be no pogroms. My Great-grandfather Kiam—
Loch Chaim—kissed the ground when he landed in New Orleans,
Kissed the body of American earth, thanked God, and set off
For the middle of Texas where a town which no longer exists
Was named after him. He celebrated Passover
Outside in the American desert of Amarillo, eating fried
Pinto beans, chili peppers and a boiled egg, which was
What there was. My mother showed me Kiam, Texas

In the 1934 Rand McNally Atlas while my sister tried
To straighten her crossed eyes by exercising them with
The stereopticon. Then we had Sunday breakfast, always
Bacon, eggs and popovers. My grandfather's wife, Fanny Tim,

A New Yorker, a German Jew, stuck a hat pin in her
Fine straw hat or her winter felt with its grosgrain ribbon
And rosette or flowers or cherries, and left to hear
John Haynes Holmes preach at the Congregational Church.

At night, the rigs burn their anointing oils to provide a halo of light
For the head of Christ. The rabbi dives into the black water,
With its rainbow patina, swimming laps after the Day of Atonement,
Struggling, like all Jews, to know the place where he lives.

A CRITICAL AGE

So that's what it's like to stand helpless at the phone,
Glasses cracked in snowflake patterns, and Information telling you
The vital numbers are unlisted. So that's what it's like
To realize you will never know what goes on behind
Closed doors, the grunts and creaking prying through the cracks,
Realize you can only know what you yourself already know.
So that's what it's like to lie helpless feeling stars of pain in
Your left side, the side you abandoned though they warned you.
So that's what it's like to win those prizes you once believed
Would provide the necessary ballast, and realize Moses
Had to find the tablets, could not tell water from stone
Within himself. Within himself, he seized on what he could,
Conviction somehow there long enough to part the sea, the waves
Of doubt. So that's what it's like to see a clear path ahead for
A moment and to know that certainty for long is like convict labor.
So that's what it's like to become weightier, as if it would keep you
Where you need to be, would provide the necessary provender.
So that's what it's like to become lighter, translucent
As a metaphor of air, to hear the music of the spheres: forte/piano,
Piano/forte—Mozart, as if on the spinet in the next room,
The windows open to those fields of particulate color.
So that's what it's like, like nothing really, beyond compare.

FOR A FRIEND WHOSE SON DROWNED

My mother called it chopmeat (my Aunt still does).
Hamburger.
I trotted along beside her, holding her hand,
my Dutch boy bob
Bobbing except for the strands glued to my head.
It was a hot July.
I dreaded naptime which would follow shopping and lunch;
the sheet would turn
To glue, too, sticking me, flushed and miserable
to the mattress.
Mr. Strook, the butcher, smiled and gave me a dollop of
chopmeat. Raw.
"Steak tartar," my mother said. "You'll like it." And I did.
My sister
Left at home with her broken leg—good, good—couldn't
talk well yet.
She could when she died two years later, but I wasn't there
to hear her,
Excluded as always from events most crucial to me.

You, too, were excluded, by circumstance, not by parents,
from the death,
Which means it comes more vividly than life—like the colors
Of L.A. twenties bungalows—
Into your dreams or nightmares, those rearing horses
that threaten us
With their steel hooves. The dream is always a variation of
the same event:
You are chopping boy, fileting boy, slicing boy:
into meatloaf, Stroganov,

Burgers with thick slices of dripping tomato on top
and parsley garnishments.
Of course this is after the death which you never see.
He is just there,
Laid out on the table, not quite cold, and pale as young veal,
almost transparent.
But when you chop there is a lot of blood which covers you
like a splatter painting.
You chop or slice or filet because you cannot let him
leave you,
Must somehow get him back inside again. You always
wake
Before the first bite to face the grey smear of the day,
hungry and insatiable.

I know all this and want to tell you I know how you feel,
want to comfort you,
To hold you and sing you songs of oblivion. You will not
allow it,
Knowing that way means losing him. Some griefs are
beyond bearing
Yet must be borne. That is what it means to bear a child.
If only
You had been there to warn him, to say, "Watch out,
watch out,"
To say, "you're not ready to ocean sail alone." And intervened.
If only
You had been there to warn him, to say, "Look out, you haven't
checked the weather."
If only you had been there to catch him in your arms, to float
together.
You walk back to bed swaying, your swollen belly, the galleon
of your loss.

Anchored in the sea of rumpled sheets, you don't know how
to mourn—
To spurn or to embrace the heavy change now he is gone.

ACCIDENTAL CAUSES

Sarah Bodner, 42, was struck by lightning today in an open field at Blessing Falls Park. Evidently she was caught unawares by the storm during a solitary picnic. She is survived by three children . . .

She wanted death, not maiming: that ruled out strolling
Country roads at night or aiming the car at a tree.
No one must know: that ruled out guns, pills,
Jumping off tall buildings. Once and only once:
That ruled out kitchen gas or car exhaust or fire,
No rescuers short-circuiting the task. She flicked
Her catalogue of deaths over and over as if
She were rehearsing *Pirates of Penzance*.

To kill yourself without a leak—the news of
Self-infliction, not of blood—is difficult if not impossible.
A flood of curiosity follows—prying, vigorous
As when shucking a good fresh oyster, as full of
Alacrity as the spinster peering through her blinds
To watch the Baptist preacher fondle the ass
Of his Chief Warden's wife. So how to seal the eyes of
The curious? Her children must not know.

She walks in the downpour. The sky has turned grey green,
As if all circulation has been stopped (the wind a tourniquet
Too long applied) and gangrene has set in. She is in the field,
Where on clear, windy days kites lace the sky,
With her picnic basket and *Anna Karenina*
(A hint, but only that) so it will look as if she has been caught
By the storm, a butterfly pinned to the green page of
The field, as, indeed, she is, has been for months.

Two storms must have converged: like lovers on dingy sheets of sky,
The bolts from north and east embrace and part and come again.
When she was four and crying, her mother took her out,
Into the rain, "Don't be afraid. The noise is just the giants bowling.
And when the great iron balls collide, it makes those fireworks."
And they had laughed and watched the grand display overhead,
All wet, yet warm and merged into their pleasure
Until her father called them in and sent her back to bed.

She stands in the field, wet and alone, holding up her arms,
Willing one bolt to leave the other and come to her,
Like any fickle lover. And when it enters her,
A lightning embrace, she almost gives the truth away,
Dying with such an ecstatic face that only grave indifference
Keeps her safe, keeps them all safe from what they do not need
To know. It is a certain form of rectitude, a certain way of
Lying which lets the living live, protected by the dying.

ROSE MAGPIE AND MAGPIE ROSE

Its unfading red petals have silvery reverses, dotted with
Dew pearls on its flaring, layered skirt, a costume for
A Busby Berkeley chorine whose colors and shimmys
Are turned to propositions by the klieg light of the full-hung
Morning sun, which seemingly attracts the magpie
Who swoops down on it, a tail-coated stage-door Johnny.
To the magpie, however, the rose is a red showcase

For jewels winking at him. He swoops down to pick up
What he sees as diamonds, pearls and rubies for his stash.
Bewildered to discover nothing that his beak can grasp,
The bird soars, higher than he rose before,
And from a distance finds again the flower's jeweled allure.
Again he dives and again finds only water,
Until the ever-stronger sun performs its prestidigitation.

Neither the magpie nor the rose can understand what went wrong
In such a passionate courtship. Marguerite, who pulled the petals
Of her namesake daisies, was equally bewildered. Deflowered,
She became Maggie, the governess, and her baby son,
Seen only once a month, became Freddie, the con man
Who took her old-age savings and ran, leaving her only
Hymns and prayers and a heart broken for the second time.

AT THE ROUND EARTH'S IMAGIN'D CORNERS: A STACK OF MARRIAGE BOXES

1. This is the mother, *a Round box, a Wrapping box, a Swaddled box,*
  This is the cradle, *a Swaddled box, a Rocking box,* a box squared.
  Then lengthened into what the rest of your life will be. The span
  Of your life, your mother's pointed fingers bridging the cradle,
  A Wrapping box, a Rocking box. When the wind blows the cradle,
  She may be there, leaning down, reaching for you, catching you
  Like a trapeze artist, like a cold, like a lover, or like a mother.

2. This is his tool box; this is a spiked box, a quilled box,
  A sharp box. He keeps it ready in his corner: naked steel,
  An axe, eelspear, oxgoad—the edge tools—a whetstone,
  Springtooth harrow, Adam's needle, a rib too sharp to
  Make a woman of, a spine, a steeple, pins, a pinnacle,
  The Chrysler building. Sing of the box of glorious spires
  And electricity. Sing of the box of spikes and spines
  Too stiff to bend. Here is the turkey buzzard, the bird of
  Jove, the basking shark and, too often, the bald eagle
  Who talks turkey and gobbles everything in sight.
  Here is the turnkey and the screw and his prick;
  This is his box, a box not of their own making.

3. This is a George III Fitted Necessaire: A high quadrangular
    Box, the hinged cover with four turtle finials and steep
    Encrusted gable roof surmounted by pine cones,
    Chased all over with rococo cartouches, embellished
    On the cover with floral festoons around beckoning hands;
    The sides with landscape vignettes, and peacock and peahen
    Amid flowering quinces and dead lilacs, drooping; the front
    With Pan playing his rush pipes while mounting a maiden
    Whose long hair sweeps around to the back where it forms
    The pubic cover of Pander arranging a liason between
    Catherine the Great and Li Po who is offering her the moon
    As a mirror. *This is a box where sweets compacted lie.*

                        4. This is the box
                          between her legs—
                            a sod house,
                           a slit of light—
                            its grass roof
                          rooting into earth,
                           vaulted darkness
                           and organ music,
                           pioneers pumping
                             the bellows.
                            This is the box
                            you need not
                          unlock—inside,
                          concentric rings
                         and New Year's Eve
                         in the fretted garden
                          of the Milky Way.
                            This is the box
                           of what is to come.

5. This is the box of his madness—a blue norther, the icy wind
Which sweeps the warm, curved landscape like a steel broom.
Temper blows the box—the place they live, the place they join—
Into fragments, the way freezing can shatter a china plate.
He stands, rueing the day of his anger, holding her heart in
His hands as if that would temper the damage. Each splitting
Norther, each blue tempest leaves a wake in its path, sadder
Than mourners can bear. They gather in a circle anyway.
In a corner the child, round white face like a china plate,
Stands   watching.

6. This is the box of her madness. She checks instructions:
How to Tattoo a Heart on His Chest: Sterilize your needles.
Check the spectrum of colored powders. Double amounts of
Red will be needed. Make sure he is the right one, the one
You can never rid yourself of. Pour black powder into
The mortar, add glycerine. Ask him how big a heart,
The colors he likes, the name of his love. Swab
His left pectoral with alcohol. Begin. Prick
The motifs in the skin, allowing room for
The artistic accident which will reveal
Your skill. Continue until blood leaks
Through the right ventricle, and
The heart convulses. Then you
Will know you are
finished.

7.   This is the sparring ring.
These are the wedding bands.
This is the music they walked down the aisle to.
These are the corners they sit in between rounds.
These are the moves they always make:
His the tango, the whirling, the dipping,
The embrace, the pressure on the neck's
Crucial spot until loss of consciousness occurs;
Hers, the becoming something else, something he
Can't grasp, a potato, peeling herself
Into the salad. The same moves over and over.
She calls, he doesn't answer. He answers,
Promises to call back, instead practices
The bagpipes. She calls him *sheepsbladder*.
He says I only play at it. He calls her *doughy*.
She says she is the staff of life.
This is the sparring ring. They are
Tired, but they go the distance again.

8.   This is a box of paralysis: if you can rise
From the chair, an indifferent father who
Holds you in his arms, walk across the room
To the box and open it, you will find it contains
Only air the shape of itself. If you cannot rise,
The musty box contains everything you must have.

9. This is the box of their love.
    A match box, a box of rice.
    What's been said once
    Will be said twice.
    This is a match box,
    A catch box. They light
    The fire. This is the box of love,
    The box of desire.
    Out there is the box of bone,
    The six-foot bungalow,
    The wooden kimono.
    In here is home,
    A box of wicker and wire
    And wool, and desire.
    This is their treasure box,
    The box of their trove,
    A wrapping box,
    A rocking box.
    This is the box of their love.

THE TRIBOROUGH BRIDGE
A CROWN FOR HIS HEAD

January day. Cold: bright vinegar rinsing clear
The East River water and sky, Welfare Island's brick,
And the winking mirrors of Queens. Clear as this month's
Particular vision: one head, two faces, which look
Forward and back to a time I count on my fingers
To remember the year, licking peach jam off them
On this Sunday morning as I sit in my pleated robe
Watching your wise Janus face looking at time—
I pray you are not otherwise two-faced—
While through the window behind you
A schoolgirl's wartime river tries to shove back
Destroyers and cruisers making their way home.
Forty-five years. *Can you count your lovers
On the fingers of two hands?* you asked last night.

Nostalgia the schoolgirl felt watching the sailors cram
The deck, waving to all of us who'd stood at the windows to
Greet them—nostalgia not for what had been experienced
But for the flood of what had not is always a threat,
A form of mild depression. Now, in first love,
For new love is always first love, the past struggles
To assert itself. My sleeve brushes the hair on your arm
As I pour coffee into your cup, the green vine pattern
Your wife picked just before she died. Only
This movement with the Dvořák quartet moving
Toward its joyful conclusion, threatening
To break the window glass, to merge air and air—
Only this moment I insist: the room and the river
Scoured clean of memory's sweet, invidious oils.

II THE PLATFORM BUILDER

The poet told me if I was serious
I must isolate myself for at least a year—
Not become a hermit, but leave
My family, job, friends—so I did. My sister
Agreed to take over as mother though not
As wife. I wonder if she will become that too;
I've always thought maybe she didn't marry
Because she wanted Howard herself. So I
Have moved here to North Dakota where
I work in a gas station, the only woman s.s.
Attendant in N.D. Nowhere could be more isolated
And no job could: whistles and "baby
Pump some of that to me" crack in the cold
Or melt in the summer.

<pre>
        try   try   try
      crycry   crycry   crycry   cry
</pre>

I have been here seven months. Poetry should
Be flowing from my navel by now, if . . .
Out of the solitude, I expected I would erect
Something magnificent, the feminine analogue
Of Jeffer's tower. Maybe it would have gone
Into the ground instead of up.

<pre>
        s   k   y
                   high
</pre>

I have discovered I drink when I am solitary. I
Have discovered I can read page ninety-two of

Remembrance of Things Past twenty times in solitary
Without ever reading it. If I don't die of alcoholism,
I will of cholesterol: solitary cooking.

  fryfryfry   fryfry   fryfryfryfry   frydie

Rhyme is important, my way of keeping
A grip on things. I wonder if the poet meant
It would all happen after I left, or if he is a sadist
Who wants to send all those stupid enough to sit
At his feet to N.D. or S.D. or West Va.,
Hazing before possible joining. I wonder if Jean
Is in the double bed.

  tower
  power

I cannot think about the children, but I
Do all the time. "Women artists fail
Because they have babies." The last thing I wrote
Was "The Children at the Beach" and that was over
A month ago. I am alone so I have to have company so
I turn on TV; at home
I only turned it off.

  thumbtacks   processionals
    north
    red

It is time to go to work. First I need a drink. I consider
The Smirnoff bottle on the coffee table; a fly
Lands on it. And then it all happens: the life
Of that bottle flashes before me. Little by little,

Or quickly, it is used up; empty, as clear as it was
Full, it journeys to the dump; it rests upon the mounds of
Beautiful excess where what we are—
Sunflowers, grass, sand—
Is joined to what we make—
Cans, tires and it itself in every form of bottle.
I put on my s.s. coveralls, a saffron robe, knowing I have found
What I was sent to find. The sky speaks to me; the sound
Of the cars on Highway 2 is a song. Soon I will see the pumps,
Those curved rectangles shaped like the U.S. and smell the gas,
Our incense. O country, O moon, O stars,
O american rhyme is yours is mine is ours.

THE PLATFORM BUILDER

If you were to construct a platform,
    That is, if you wanted to construct a platform
  And then you did (after a lot of self-instruction
      On platform building and frequent consultation
  With the building supply people) and you worked
    Weekends till your friends, unobsessed with platforms,
    Stopped calling. And if, then, you finally got it built,
With what an invasion of accomplishment you'd view it . . . The tools
Not even put away, but left beside the scaffolding,
    You'd buy three things you'd been wanting and thinking about
                                         buying
    And sit with an old friend to watch "The Shoeshine Boy" on TV
If it was on.

The next day, looking at your platform,
    You'd see the gap between the second and third planks
      And how the miters showed how many
    Times you had made corrections. If you made
Another platform, you'd fix those things. And in the thinking of
                                      another
      The need is there or maybe the need
      Made you think of it.
So you begin again. Of course, it is more difficult,
    Demanding a platform cantilevered on the first,
      A kind of step above a base.
You build it, with the foreseen result: like owners who correct
In every house they build the faults of the last one; the flaws are not
The same, but there are flaws.

With each successive platform, the skill increases
    And the demands increase beyond the increase of the skills;
The choice of wood, fitting without nails or glue, the curve
        To change direction at the sixteenth level
        When, emerging above the trees, it's evident
        The direction chosen affords a view
Of the oil storage tanks instead of the sea.
And then, a few levels higher, the question whether wood at all
    Or plexiglass (acrophobia?) or steel (too cold in winter?),
    Etc. And, on the twenty-second level, having to stop completely
        For Zoning Board appeals because you've gone
Beyond the allowed height for an AA zone.
        And interviews, and manufacturers who want you to build
    Another just the same, using their product.

Young builders, contemplating platforms,
        Examine what you've done and ask you how
You did those first ones and sometimes you say you can't remember,
        Which is true, and sometimes you try
To think just how and answer with how you did the latest ones
    Or even how you think you're going to do the next,
If you find time to do it.
    And they imagine you content with, not so much what you've
                                                        made—
        They've heard of creative dissatisfaction—
    But that it's been accepted; that you can get money and more
Than money for a speech on "How I Build Platforms" and only
        Will be asked to set another date
If you get drunk and don't show up.

If you want to build a platform, and ask for my advice,
        I'll give it, but remember
    I can't remember back to where you are . . .

I think I would use wood to start,
   To get the platform's natural connection.
White ash is strong and tough and has escape built in its name.
      I think I cannot say it better than to say
If I were about to start to build a platform,
I think I'd start with ash.

THE TUNE HE SAW

Woods. A stand, waiting for the bite, the teeth.
Joshua Briggs picks logs from the stack he's cut,
Sticks them in the black belly, fixing dinner—
Pork, beans and slaw—before the night's concert.
Tunes shimmy in pieces. He looks out at his lot, his stand of
Woods. Notes the green. That shine.
"Play a tune on a jug; the moon pops out like a cork.
But that's nothing to playing a saw."

He puts in his teeth for the slaw. Sweet sap, molasses,
Spreads around hillocks of salt pork into it.
The Moonlight Sonata hangs over his head.
And the light of the saw. "You can use it to cut, too.
That very same instrument." His parcel of
Woods. Pieces of green; the notation of trunks and
The land, that ground bass over which his
Single strand of tune will soar like an angel.

"Lots of people my age like a tune.
Today it's all beat but I give them music."
He begins to practice. The saw bends.
Quavering moonlight fills the room. The saw
Arches and twists between hand and thigh.
He strokes it with his bow, "A cello bow made
From manes of white Argentine horses. That country's got
Silver in its name." The saw angles and dips
Like a waterfall between hand and thigh.

The semi-, demi-, hemi-quavers, the crotchets of
Wood are joined as Joshua Briggs

Bends what he saw. The tune rises like the holy ghost.
It will rise, that Moonlight Sonata,
Above the audience at the Grange
Like the host. He will greet them with music.
His white forelock falls over his eyes as he bows, twisting
Silver between hand and thigh.
He describes the tune in the air, sawing it into
Parcels of light. "Angels are women; I know that."
The room is full of what he can accept.

THE LADY PITCHER

It is the last of the ninth, two down, bases loaded, seventh
Game of the Series and here she comes, walking
On water,
Promising miracles. What a relief
Pitcher she has been all year.
Will she win it all now or will this be the big bust which
She secures in wire and net beneath her uniform,
Wire and net like a double
Vision version
Of the sandlot homeplate backstop in Indiana where
She became known as Flameball Millie.

She rears back and fires from that cocked pistol, her arm.
Strike one.
Dom, the catcher, gives her the crossed fingers sign,
Air, but she shakes it off and waits for fire.
Strike two.
Then the old familiar cry, "Show them you got balls, Millie."
But she knows you should strike while the iron is hot
Even though the manager has fined her
Sixteen times for disobeying
The hard and fast one:
A ball after two strikes.
She shoots it out so fast
It draws
An orange stripe on that greensward.
Strike three.

In the locker room they hoist her up and pour champagne
All over her peach satin, lace-frilled robe.
She feels what she has felt before,
The flame of victory and being loved
Moves through her, but this time
It's the Series and the conflagration matches
The occasion.

In the off-season she dreams of victories and marriage,
Knowing she will have them and probably not it.
Men whisper, in wet moments of passion,
"My little Lowestoft," or, "My curvy Spode," and
They stroke her handle, but she is afraid that yielding means
Being filled with milk and put on
The shelf;
So she closes herself off,
Wisecracking.
When she is alone again she looks at the china skin
Of her body, the crazing, the cracks she put there
To make sure
She couldn't
Hold anything for long.

11 A.M.   Arthur Nikisch took my chin in his hand
And said, one day you will be my Eva.
Now, they have not even heard of Nikisch
And my chin is doubled . . . Yes, Minouchou, I'm coming.
Mon petit Chou, you want your fresh chicken
Liver. You dream of liver floating in
White cream, Chou-chou? Jane, you'll have to wait while
I go downstairs to shop. Back in four, or
At most five, minutes . . . Min-ou-chou! Bad girl!
How could you? Let me see it, Jane. We must
Wash it with soap. Wait, I'll put her in *there*.
So, so sorry. She gets a terrible anger
When she is hungry, like Santuzza
Spitting at the tenor . . . Here: this is a German
Disinfectant which truly disinfects.
The retired wig mistress at Stuttgart
Sends me a jar each December. Which makes
Me remember that Fritz Knoedler used to say
Wicks Wapo Roob. He could not pronounce the
Double U . . . Yes? Thank you . . . Well, I studied English
With hard study. The diction is a tool.

NOON   Yes, Martha, I heard it . . . Yes, she was quite
Pretty, but not sufficient dramatisch.
You know in Act Two, Leonora has
Left the world of earthly love behind her;
She sings now to the stars, thick as weeds in
A warm summer field, and to the angels
Who hold them. You must feel this in her prayer,
Not that she kneels to pray for good high C's.

If I could sing now, I would sing it now
Even better than I once did. "Madre,
Pietosa Virgine." Better than when
Olin Downes wrote—quote: "Her Leonora
Was so beautiful that for once Verdi's
Soaring was matched by the singer's singing."
The New York Times, March third, 1940.
"Madre, pietosa . . . when I hear it float
Toward the flies, my heart aches to sing again.

2 P.M.   No, Christopher, the scale down even. I
Want the same time on each note and the same
Volume top to bottom . . . Your voice sounds weak
Today . . . Dieting! Terrible. You wish
To sing Walter or a thin spargel like
Beckmesser? I will fix you a healthy
Drink right away. You must eat sensible . . .
Here—no milk; it is bad for the voice like
Glue for the chords. Very few know that dieting was
What ruined Marian Talley so young.
Now, after five minutes we again start.

3 P.M.   That is not how it should be. Remember
She is an innocent girl who cannot
Believe he, he the most wonderful of
Men has chosen her, her who is nothing.
So you must make the dotted sixteenths sharp,
Not sloppy eighths . . . Yes, yes, much better, but
Be alive while I play the prelude. She
Is shy, not dead . . . You see him before your
Eyes, "Er der Herrlichste von Allen"; his
Blue eyes flash. Your hands move to your breast. Sway
Gently the innocent sway—sorry—four
Flats is difficult for me. Again please.

4 P.M.   Today, I want to go through the whole of
Dichterliebe. But exercises first . . .
Too nasal. Imagine you are biting
An apple with your uvula . . . Better . . . Ja, but
Still more space: make the apple a melon . . .
Good. Good. I think we can begin . . . What is it
Named—this song? . . . Correct. But I don't
Feel the impatience. "Dein ist mein Herz. Dein
Ist mein Herz," must mount impetuously.
Like Octavian in the first act of
Rosenkavalier. Lotte Himmelblau
Was the greatest Octavian there has
Ever been. And I say this even though
I sang the role myself when I was young,
Before I sang the Marschallin. We have
Done over eight-hundred performances
Together of Der Rosenkavalier.
She was so handsome, so impetuous.
We always played Scene I in bed, but in
America the Metropolitan
Insisted on a couch. Ridiculous.
They have just awoken from a night of
Passion. Did they sleep on the narrow couch?
In Vienna, we did it as Strauss wished:
Only my hand and arm, like a rose sprung
From a nest of lace, my nightgown sleeve, could
Be seen through the open silk bed curtains.
She was truly my Quinquin. In that role,
I sang my Metropolitan farewell,
Although I had retired six years
Before from opera. Mr. Johnson begged
Till I agreed to come back for one
Last performance. Even the ushers

49

Had wept and thrown flowers at my final
Previous farewell. It is a role one
Can sing with less voice, though the last act
Has demanding tessitura for all three.
Lottchen came backstage, but she couldn't sing
Then, not even Lieder—too much wobble.
Though we sang longer than they now do
Because our *vocal foundation was sound*—
No fly-by Callases. But it was sad
To sing with another Octavian
In my arms when it was my true farewell,
But more sad for Lotte, who was brave and
Stayed until the very end after they
Had brought the fire curtain down three times . . .
No . . . it is nothing . . . But, I'm sorry, we
Have no more time. A minute while I will
Look at my book . . . See you Saturday at
Five . . . Don't worry . . .

"Die alte Frau, die alte Marschallin,
Da geht die alte . . ." Here, Chou. Come here, Chou-Chou;
Du bist mein Schatz, Chou. Ich hab' Dich lieb.

ANOTHER ATTEMPT AT THE TRICK

Once the basic skills have been mastered
Our only enemy is uncertainty. In the act,
Even in the name to waver is to
    Trip. For instance: tightrope walker, a trifle awkward,
    But not until I thought of it did I discover
    R falling over W; and now my tongue
    Is always twisted by the word. You see
    You cannot say it once you
    Think about the process. And once you've thought you
                          cannot

Say you will not think and stop your thoughts.
    The act of will defeats itself. And so, I fell
    In my final trial run . . . or walk.
        Perhaps the feat—no, not the feet—
    Failed or was defeated by my hesitation.
But I am getting tangled up again.

  What I had planned to do was this:
To play the last movement of Beethovens' Pathétique Sonata
    On the mid-point above Niagara Gorge.
    You see there is a grand tradition of tight-
Rope walking across the gorge,
    But this performance would have been something
    Quite unique. A tightrope man who is besides a skilled
                        pianist;
    Well, that is something new. And then simply to get
The piano from the platform to the center demands a degree
    Of strength and balance beyond the norm. I had done it
Two weeks before at Quechee Gorge, but what had happened
Then should have given me pause: my memory lapsed

About half-way through the movement and lapsed again
       Each time I started over, until I simply had to stick
A dominant-tonic on and stop as if it were the end,
    Which it was not, of course, but which it should have been.
        So two weeks later I paused and fell. I will not
       Go into the quarrels with my wife which came
Before the fall. Or tell in detail
        How they weakened my confidence.
   It is enough to say I fell.

           They had to amputate
           But it was neat,
           Just below both knees;
           So I am now four feet
           Instead of six feet tall,
           Like Ferrer as Lautrec,
           Except I really walk
           On booted knees. You
           Marvel at my attitude?
           Well, I have had four
        Years in which to become detached.

And so the preamble concludes; the postamble
Begins. After a year in the hospital to heal
Internal injuries and train with my prosthetic feet,
I came home. My wife had found a job and with
My workman's compensation we could manage;
So it was not for money alone that I agreed
To teach the bearded lady. It was compassion,
A quality which comes with pain, or came for me.
She was losing the hair on her chin and as she'd had
Some tightrope training as a child wanted
To take it up as an alternative profession.

It was hard to build up her skill as fast as her hair fell out,
  But she was diligent and I compulsive
 And by the time a small curled fall
      Attached with spirit gum could no longer conceal
Her sparseness of beard, she was nearly ready,
      Totally ready in terms of what your average tightrope
                                    walker
   Can do, but she was my pupil and average
      Was not enough. She couldn't play piano
         So that was out. I tell you that we agonized
         A lot to find that special thing. And then we never really
         Found it. It happened. I got divorced
And married her and she got pregnant. We both
      Knew right away a pregnant tightrope walker
         Was unique. I wish you could have seen her balance
            In the later months with that huge bulge in front;
   The crowds were absolutely quiet during the act
  But when she finished her headstand
  And Rock-a-bye-baby ended with a fanfare
      The noise was louder than Niagara Falls.

      That this act had a built-in date for finishing
      Is evident. But we were ready, though not ready
   For the answer to a tightrope walker's prayers:
            Twins, the pairing for two arms, two breasts, two
                                    buttocks,
         Two legs upon a single wire. Every night she walks,
            Balancing babies, they and she the product
   Of, respectively, my semen and my skill. I call myself
  Thrice blessed and only sometimes worry
That she may hesitate. So far she never
Has. She never

            Has.

THE SECRETS OF E. MUNCH

What showed
In the agonized O of the mouth,
The open arms like knives,
The paint thick as spoiled cream
Was his public secret;
The private one,
Concealed like pubic hair,
Was his love of Grieg,
That other Edvard. Music
Full of girls in white lawn dresses on lupine-studded meadows,
Of blond young men in blue velvet suits, sweetly philandering,
Of suns, fresh as newly hung laundry, rising and rising.
All tensions, the slight pains of D major,
Twinges of A minor, quickly solved in
Tender resolutions.

Grieg pursued him even when he locked
The pianoforte.
Grieg forced him to evident mutilations.
No one would notice as he
Bled through his gloves onto the canvas
That he hummed "The Violet Who Loved the Shepherd."

THE STAINED GLASS MAN

Professor Oakes Ames
Director, Botanical Museum
Harvard University
Cambridge, Mass.

*Dear Professor Ames, It seems easiest in this very long letter to
separate the description of the glass work from the more per-
sonal part; so I have done this, and will tell you about the making of the models later. I have been out to Hosterwitz, half an
hour by auto and have passed two whole afternoons, long ones,
looking at the models. Then I inspected the work room and its
contents and was shown all the great improvements made by
the Blaschkas in the house since his marriage.*

I have found, my dear Miss Ware, a new way of coloring the glass
Since you were here in 1908. I use no surface paint at all;
See this budding rose. You could leave it on the roof a year;
The shading would not change a micrometer. I know because I have
Done exactly that. The color is in the glass. Layer after
Layer I build it up. Not one, but many, like light itself.

> *I think he said he no longer paints at all except with the pow-
> dered colored glass which he can anneal.*

Here a sheet of cashew lake and one of violet beneath the luteous
Combine to form yellow of high intensity and brilliance,
A requirement of this liliaceous group. Their cups contain
The sun of early June, radiant, but with a touch of cooling blue.

> I am covered with leaves. Leaves I have made.
> They stick to me, annealed by the heat of

Loneliness. I am covered with glass
Of my own making. Leaves. The leavings.
The parting. The final leaving. The left-overs.

The green of this ligulate corolla contains a drop of milk,
A happy accident, the accident for which a long apprenticeship
Prepares one. One day I ate, or at that moment drank would be
More accurate, my lunch while searching for a way to soften color
At the junction of the blade and petiole. You ascertain
The rest without the tale. You see the milky green.

*He is just as modest and honorable as he ever was, but now he
has a sense of his own worth, his own unusual force of intellect
and character; and there is everything to justify that.*

I regret this group of fungi is not complete for I can
Only do them as and when I can obtain the specimens.
My old gatherer died at sixty-eight three months ago and then
The new one died of tasting, though I warned him. The smuts and
   rusts
I grow here, but the mushrooms I must leave to someone else.

Rusting, Rusting. Spores through skin.
Molds forming skin. Molds.
   Molds stiffening. The marriage mold becomes
The man. The armor.
   Close to cupid's sound, but further than
The new moon shining: a cutlass,
   A scimitar, a blade,
      Slashing the air between us,
   Cutting, parting.

*The molds are wonderful, and I think you will be delighted
with them all, but, of course, I know nothing of fungi.*

56

The problem with Laver is it spoils when removed from the sea.
Its purples drain. It browns.
Fluidity becomes flaccidity. So I have had to work looking
Through the double barrier of glass and water. You would say
Both are clear, but clarity is an illusion.

*Mr. Blaschka's head and bearing are very expressive and I wished
I could catch a photograph of his profile as he stood for a few
minutes, a plaque with a model on it held with both hands. His
whole expression of absorbed, concentrated study was worth
keeping, had it been possible.*

Now, the land grasses. The lemma here, the lower bract—
Enclosing as it does the flowers in the spikelet of the grass—
Is smooth and tousled. I see a field of wheat within
This single stalk before me as I work.

Transplanting them to the museum is
The next-to-sharpest agony. Another
Parting. Worse by far than
The splinter of glass
Under the nail. It is the pain of sudden
Feeling come too late. O, Lilianne,
I dream you have not left.
I keep the Boecklin *Flora* over the mantel.
The keeping, the keeping. The dreaming.
The parting.

You are most kind: supper and *Der Freischütz* are indeed
A lure. But I must put the next-to-final touch on the asparagus.
These stalklets will have lost their velvet by tomorrow.
Now the flowerets curve in like cat's claws holding to
The branch. There is a desperation of the parts within the flame.

It troubles me very much that he and his wife cannot come over to see his life's work now that you have the models so beautifully arranged, and he looks so eager and pathetic when I describe the mise en scène.

This is the laver where I wash away the residues before
I trace the veins. Bronze. Because a brazen vessel clarifies
The light without refraction. Now, I will show you how
I do the leaf annealing. Cups of paraffin. I light them till
The flames drive at each other. This lever moves the apparatus.
The tips in first, then, bit by bit, the whole until it all turns
Red, as the after-image of a leaf stared at in sunlight.
And then the turning and the twisting for vein and edge.

> Lilianne, I tell this all to you.
> I speak to you whether I am silent
> Or talk aloud. The rest
> Is only the fragment of the whole. Like half
> A phrase of the Schubert we heard
> The night you left.
> Or like that single leaf. There.
> On the red crepe pillow.
> Single.
> The turning, the twisting.
> Single. The seeing. The parting.

The strawberries were fascinating—plants, fruit and molds: also the result of frost on the developing fruit.

> The strawberries, my strawberries.
> Clustered like the nipples of Venus.
> Of Aphrodite. To suck. To bite.
> I picture babies crying at the case,

58

Their milk need roused by my rosy artifacts.
I picture you,
Lilianne, holding the baby.
Smiling. Rocking. Holding.

My last visit to Hosterwitz was most happy. Miss Niklason went
with me and enjoyed it as much as I did. Supper was excellent,
informal and pleasant, and I regaled them with all the Museum
gossip I could think up. Mr. Blaschka did some leaf work again
and Miss N. felt, just as I do, that it is a great experience to
watch that man at work. His whole head and hands are a study,
and he worked until it was about dark without turning on his
electric light. She also felt that the work was enough to wear
anyone's nerves to madness.

You said you would not have me.
Encased in glass. Encasing.
Now I make what I make from
The material of myself.
The leaving, the parting.
Then the loving.
Within my case I drown.
The leaving. The parting. The living.
Drawn out. Long drawn out. What works
Is work. Look at me.
It is all clear.

I know it has given him fresh courage to see me. I have been
out there five times and I am sure that I accomplished what I
came for. Please remember me to Louis and, with most cordial
greetings to you and Mrs. Ames,
Very sincerely yours,
Mary Lee Ware

Because as they cut it was that special green, they decided
To make a woman of the fresh hay. They wished to lie in green, to wrap
Themselves in it, light but not pale, silvered but not grey.
Green and ample, big enough so both of them could shelter together
In any of her crevices, the armpit, the join
Of hip and groin. They—who knew what there was to know, about baling
The modern way with hay so you rolled it up like a carpet,
Rather than those loose stacks—they packed the green body tight
So she wouldn't fray. Each day they moulted her to keep her
Green and soft. Only her hair was allowed to ripen into yellow tousle.

The next weeks whenever they stopped cutting they lay with her.
She was always there, waiting, reliable, their green woman.
She gathered them in, yes she did,
Into the folds of herself, like the mother they hadn't had.
Like the women they had had, only more pliant, more graceful,
Welcoming in a way you never just found.
They not only had the awe of taking her,
But the awe of having made her. They drank beer
Leaning against the pillow of her belly
And one would tell the other, "Like two Adams creating."
And they marveled as they placed
The cans at her ankles, at her neck, at her wrists so she
Glittered gold and silver. They adorned what they'd made.
After harrowing they'd come to her, drawing
The fountains of the Plains, the long line
Of irrigating spray and moisten her up.
And lean against her tight, green thighs to watch buzzards
Circle black against the pink stain of the sunset.

What time she began to smolder they never knew—
Sometime between night when they'd left her
And evening when they returned. Wet, green hay
Can go a long time smoldering before you notice. It has a way
Of catching itself, of asserting that
There is no dominion over it but the air. And it flares suddenly
Like a red head losing her temper, and allows its long bright hair
To tangle in the air, letting you know again
That what shelters you can turn incendiary in a flash.
And then there is only the space of what has been,
An absence in the field, memory in the shape of a woman.

III INHERITANCE

A FAMILY OF DOLLS' HOUSE DOLLS

The mother and father do not get along.
She is dressed in pink velvet; he
In a brown suit. The house is called a Dutch
Colonial. The living room has a secretary and
A carpet like moss. There are two medium-
Size children, both girls. Everyone
Has blue eyes and they are all blonde except
The father who has light brown hair. They bend
Quite well, though they are not jointed. I think
They are wired. Most of the time they fight. The sisters
About who interrupted who and which
Toy belongs to which of them. They try
To pull out each other's hair, but it
Is firmly rooted. Their room is yellow and white
And frilled with organdy the way I wish mine was.
They kick each other almost every time they
Are awake and would be lumped and bruised if
They were not composition. Maybe I will paint
Black and blues on one. Perhaps if they
Had friends they would not always fight. I have asked
For friends, but I will have to wait until
Next Christmas, unless my grandmother brings them when
She comes to visit. The dining room has a chandelier
As sparkling as an earring. There is a maid, but she
Is too big to play with them. She really
Cannot do anything but be a maid.
I cut a hole in a wash cloth and made her a dress,
But the white maid-hat is part of her composition hair;
So you could see she was still the maid.
She is always complaining about her varicose veins. The hall

Wallpaper is the color of sky. I am not
Exactly sure why the mother and father do not
Get along. They fight sometimes about who
Interrupted who or why someone
Invested too much in something or whether they
Will be too early or too late for the dinner
Party. But mostly they do not fight, but also
They do not get along. The bathroom has
A tub and basin and toilet and towels, but no
Water. She is very beautiful, especially
When she wears her diamond earrings. Her children
Come in when she is dressing to go out
And watch her put them on. She is really
Beautiful. The father would be all right looking
Except his nose is too big. But he
Is smart. He can always answer most things
And when he cannot he says, "Let's look it up," and
Gets a book from their brown library right away
To look it up in, even in the middle of dinner
When the maid is just passing him the platter.
He never says anything nice about
The mother, even when she wears her earrings.
Except once when he and his children were
Looking out the window to see when she
Would come home he saw her in the distance
And they said, "How do you know it's her?"
Because she was still too far away to tell,
And he said, "I know her walk." That
Is as near saying something good about her
As he ever has. The lights really turn on
And off. If I thought it would help, I would ask for a new
Father for Christmas, but they come in pairs and what
Would I do with the new mother? Maybe she could be

A governess. But I do not know if the new father
Would be any different. There is a loaf of bread
In the bread box and red celluloid flames in the fireplace.

MISTRESS MARY QUITE CONTRARY

"If the artist abandons himself to his feeling, color presently announces itself."

Goethe's Color Theory

Because she had been born in February, the coldest month,
And in a cold house, the juggler had been
Perfecting her act since early childhood when she had kept
Two nipples from her bottles in the air at the same time.
She needed to, even though they had said not to,
And would not buy extras, and the shortage of milk
Made her bones soften.

Seven years after she had joined Ringling Bros.,
She was kissed by the ringmaster before she went on
To perform a new number for the first time:
Sixteen bells blindfolded while buried
In a tank of snow up to her neck. Using only
Her forearms and hands, she circled silver bells
To the arched sky. She felt them changing.
Color flowed through her fingers like blood
Returning after freezing. Taking off her blindfold
As they pulled her
Out to bow, she saw
The blue of hyacinths, the red of tulips,
The yellow of daffodils, the purple of iris, the green.
Spring had fallen into her hands. There was
No holding it back.

THE MOTHER OF THE SUN

He was born the sun. Hair (yes, his inheritance),
Golden corona, face, flat and luminous.
"A clock," said the nurse
Holding him up by his hands,
But the doctor, who knew the family, said,
"No. The sun." They named him Ray, the Sun Prince,
Because Sonnenheim was wrong for exhibition:
"Behold the sun, living like ordinary royalty,
Taking a bath, Sleeping. Eating his floating island."

He was impossible to hold.
His mother, who loved him most,
Who knew that her light would come from him after
His father died, could not resist him
And her arms and breasts were covered with burns.

Finally she had to leave him; she had her own
Course to follow. The Rival Circus insisted,
Ignoring her protest that she would be
Nothing without reflection, a sequin in the dark.
They had bought her contract and wanted
Their Queen Diane.
All she could do was lie, pale on the table like
A grey plate, no matter
How much gold lamé they surrounded her with.

Until the day he brought his baby to see her:
The son of the sun.
When she bent to kiss him,
The years of separation had lowered her resistance

And she caught fire, burning, a new meteor
Trailing blue and
Orange ribbons of flame. She burned her way
Right through the tobacco canvas of the main tent
And ignited the night sky over
The western Sun Belt like a match on black paper.

In five minutes she had almost devoured herself
And went out, leaving only splinters which
Would fall some day like knives into
The earth. The father threw his son up in
The air, saying, "My mother is there, playing
Hide and seek,
Waiting for you. Kiss
The sky. Maybe she will come back to us."

But she hid behind a veil of milk;
The star of her own show.

They were looking (as they still looked at the flag and
Other residual emblems, feeling a crinkle
Of lost certainties) for someone to show he knew
What they needed. And I, who had three times tried
To kill myself but each time was saved by a quirk,
Decided I was being saved for something. I asked
Myself was I to be the one they looked for?
To answer that question, I applied for grants
From four foundations. Fluent as I am in Yakut,
Chuckchee and Manangkabau—the only man I know of
Fluent in all three—I was able to choose the grant
I chose to analyze how the glottal manipulations
And palate shape of the three tongues affected
The development of their mathematical systems.
I thought I would hurry through my monograph
And spend the time on studying myself. But while
I delved into the rites which ultimately shaped
The tongues which shaped their mathematical
Systems, I found I had found myself before I had looked.

To summarize that initial summary: the man
Who is to lead the village receives a sign
He is being saved from death by a former shaman
Who returns from the bowl of heaven to the plate
Of earth in the guise of an animal. I saw Fred
Breaking the window in his hawk costume the night
Of the Bat Masque as I lay in the gas-filled kitchen.
And then the day I jumped off the ledge and was
Saved from death on the rocks by a blanket of seals.
One large one in particular prevented my shattering.

And finally (and this you can't dismiss as circumstance)
What happened at the third attempt: I tried
To throw myself in front of the A train of the IND.
The train rushed toward me, growing enormously, ready
To meet me. Then, just as I pushed off the edge,
A hand lifted me back, a voice said: Do not fear
The universe. I turned to face my savior, my
Betrayer and saw an almost Oriental, exceptionally tall
For an Oriental, if he was, wearing a blue sweatshirt
Lettered in white: LUMA. Not an animal,
You say? I didn't think so either till,
Examining a Yakut funeral chant, I found
Their shaman's name: Luma, meaning soul-bird.

Once I had deciphered the first meanings
Of the shaman's messages to me, subsequent
Translation accelerated like the breaking
Of a code. I knew now I had been chosen.
But exactly for what and how? The first step,
At any rate, was clear. I discussed mechanics
With the p.r. firm of Schluss and Yamaguchi.
We all agreed that, to save time at the time
When my mission would be revealed,
We should devise a scheme to dramatize
My ability to lead. Techniques which work
In a small settlement, the usual shaman abode,
Cannot be used in country-wide dissemination.

I thought of it myself—I'd walk through fire,
Not just a flaming hoop, but lots.
The p.r. men congratulated me and arranged
To have it televised (prime time) before a studio
Audience. I assured them I had done it many times

Before, which was not true. But I had put myself
Through other tests—sleeping in a nest of snakes,
Walking over ice so thin those following fell through.
To fit myself for the ordeal, I read the fire-thought
Of holy men and worked on pain in trance.
I got so that six-inch nails through both
Palms were simply pure white light.

The day came. The Schluss and Yamaguchi ads
Announcing the firewalk had engrossed the nation.
I was assigned my own mailbag, I got so many letters.
They asked advice, sent me money for my cause,
Wrote of love, both physical and spiritual.
I had to disconnect the phone. That afternoon,
Before the walk, I tested my immunity by passing
A deerskin image of myself through the flame
Of my gas stove. It did not burn or even darken;
So I was confident, able to nap before air-time.

The fire was before me, a solid field
Of it, forty by forty feet. I was afraid.
The atmosphere was difficult for trance.
I stared at the TV spots, widening my pupils
Till I soared, a soul-bird. The lights became
The sun, bright, white, dissolving my body,
Moving me through the void into the flame.
It burned. The pain was wordless, beyond
Screaming, telling or retelling. I knew
I could not do it. But I was past the center,
The point of no return.

I have limited
Use of one

Foot with which
I am writing.
Half the day
I lie on air,
A new technique
Used here to treat
Third-degree
Burn cases. It is
A form of levitation
Worthy of a more
Effective shaman.
The other half
I try to sleep
On sheepskin.
My bones protrude;
My country has not made it through the fire.

INHERITANCE

I see my mother's last breath
Which has not been drawn
In pen and ink, its jagged graph scrawled on my face,
Crossing out my features
With her lines.
Her lines come out of my mouth so that I discuss
The appearance of the neighbor's children,
The dirty streets of New York
And love, in the same tone of smooth disapproval.
Disapproval sours
My skin into hers,
Implants her congealed brown eyes, her long nose to
Look down, her lips
Like the edges of oysters.

Once a day I sandpaper my features. The swelling
Has obliterated both of us. The basin
On my lap catches our common blood.

The nylon crescent of her pink panties hangs in the sky
And I can't slip on anything or into
Something comfortable because Mama always told me
"You're the man now, now he's gone. Be a good boy,"
But I wouldn't turn down a green silk robe or a bed
Because Mama, listen to me, you know I do wear the pants.

The others were jealous because I was born under
A special moon with the great scorpion rising
And ram horns battering the smeary streak
Of milk in black sky like a needle in
A Carmen Dios record and today I wore grey ones over khakis
Over my jeans because it is cold for July.

And they were jealous because I went to school
And got a round, gold medal and because I knew so much
That they sliced the watermelon into halves like a moon
With that green rim giving warning and they seeded
The dark pink flesh with something because they were jealous
And they wanted me stupid the way they were.

And I bit into the flesh of the melon moon
And Perdita danced for me in her shiny yellow skirt
And I knew I was slipping down Truxillo Street
As if it were a banana peel and broke every bone in my body.
But they didn't get me stupid. All I can see
Is the nylon crescent of her pink panties hanging
On the post on my bed and I keep asking—can't you hear—
When can I see my Mama?

THE LATE MOTHER

One, two, Buckle my shoe
      To go to Boston.
      The phone call said she was going:
      "She can't last long," but
      The buckle has come off my shoe.
Three, four, Close the door.
      Thread the needle.
      There are tears and I am getting
      Far-sighted.
      Try again.
      Knot the thread and sew the buckle on.
Five, six, Pick up sticks.
      Five years ago she almost set the bed on fire,
      Hiding her cigarette under the blanket
      When the surgeon came.
      He took out her lung.
      I have sewn the buckle on backwards.
      Is she puffing away now, blowing
      Smoke out of her tracheotomy tube
      Like the billboard man
      Who steamed rings over Times Square?
Seven, eight, Don't be late.
      I am ripping off the buckle.
      As soon as I finish I will go.
      I will not be late for the dying. Probably.
      The thread knots binding me to my place.
      My father said to her, "We are going to be late
      For the dinner party." Then she said it
      To her next husband, as if
      The going out must be a struggle.

Nine, ten, Big, fat hen,
>Warm and feathery,
>A nest of softness.
>Never was, could not be,
>"Teach her to tie her shoes, Mademoiselle.
>She can't seem to learn and I must
>Dress for the dinner party."
>The buckle is on.
>I keep the needle threaded in case.

>The rhyme is over.
>We must leave the nursery
>But we are afraid.
>I hold her, eighty pounds, in my arms,
>Becoming her mother and my own.

It was a gray day; the dogs were barking.
Big Jill Sprat, née Horner
Sat in a corner, sticking her thumb in
Because she knew she was alone. The plum
Was dark and juicy, but the only man
She had ever loved
Was Jack, not her husband, Jack, but her brother,
Jack, who had sold his stock, left her and town
And gone to London to blow his horn,
While she was left alone with Sprat
Who kept telling her she was overweight,
But ate all the lean and left her
The fat, curds and whey, and pease porridge hot;
So no wonder. The doctor said no wonder
Because she was pregnant, that after nine days
She would deliver from her pot
A bone. Her maternity dress was velvet,
Dark and seductive, but she was alone.
It was a gray day; the dogs were barking.
The beggars were coming to a town of beggars.

When Priss is in Virginia, she is very careful not
    To fall apart. Her father, whose grandfather changed his name from
Levy to Lee, taught her that the birthplace of presidents induces
    A state of caution, knowing that family trees can be
Dangerous as standing under one in lightning storms and the bough
    Breaks and the cradle falls and you have to be *so* careful
Of a baby sister. So she is very careful not to fall apart,
    Poking Virginia's mouth to make sure she has no teeth.
Priss *was* careful even though Virginia cried.
    The columns of Virginia's addition were neat as Mount Vernon's
Although she was cross-eyed because she got a weak muscle which was
    Too bad and made it hard to tell she was telling the truth
When Priss lied and bit her arm and said Virginia'd done it.

    Imperfection, as we all know, is looked at askance in
First families especially those with impeccable new names so
    Even when she is not in Virginia she is very careful,
Remembering particularly the dismembered doll and its consequences.
    Her father said the undertaker said Virginia was beautiful
In her coffin though he wouldn't look and had her
    Sealed up. But Virginia is beautiful even when she falls apart
Though Priss disdains her state as if Priss were the DAR denying
    Constitution Hall. Realize, though, Virginia
Is not the first family because she is the father's second wife
    And look! Virginia is falling apart. Pearls of tears form
In the socket cups where her eyes rest like grey oysters.

How painful it must be to extrude a pearl. Like a gallstone,
Priss imagines as if she did not know. Pretty Virginia with
  Her round hill breasts and curves and rivers and breathy bays.
Pretty Virginia, so pretty with her calm face like a doll's,
  The head of a doll in a puddle on the roof where
You could look across the street at the Lenox Hill interns lying
  On the beds of the nurses with the nurses and, oh dear,
Virginia is falling and this time Priss cannot look because
  There is something in her eye, a piece of grit or soot
Which must be lacquered over because only Virginia who falls
  Is allowed to though she must have been put back together
Because see, see she is stretching her arms languidly and smiling
  With her perfect teeth at someone, but Priss cannot quite
Make out who when there is still something in her eye. The muscle of

  Bivalves' shells is so extraordinarily strong
It is called a catch. It is extraordinarily difficult to
  Pry it open, to slide the shucking knife into
Its tight mouth. Her father has extraordinary skill. At the mouth
  Of the Rappahannock he holds Virginia in his arms,
Shucking knife at his feet, holding her together, preparing
  Like Priss preparing for yet another Virginia, supposing,
As we all do, that this casual meeting is unsullied by others,
  That there will be only the protecting translucent sheet
Through which she will see as sharply as the meticulous oyster knife
  Slices the muscle's lock, and will not be left to wonder
Why she loves some stranger to the quick, why she takes her
  To herself and why the translucent sheet turns
Opaque in the middle of a sentence like mica thickly layered:
  Sparkling, attracting, reflecting back Priss in Virginia.

DEPARTURE

When he cut off his feet I knew he was leaving . . .
A mother's instinct. He sat a moment allowing
The ankle stumps to heal, then walked out the front door.
I didn't try to stop him; I knew he had to go—
Everyone said so. He left me his feet; I
Treasured them because now they had to be all of him.
I felt the toes for messages, crying
Over the corrugated toenails which had always tended
To become ingrown. How many times I had notched
Those nails to ease a swollen corner. I stroked
The skin, touching the rest of his body. I kissed the heels.

He sent me postcards of the Corn Palace, the Mormon Tabernacle,
The Astrodome and Mt. Rainier where he says he
Will stay for a while. I mounted the cards
Above the gilt table which holds the velvet-lined box
Containing the feet. He has left me alone
With souvenirs and my spondees.

Want ad in the *Mt. Rainier Gazette:* Come back, Scott,
Mother misses you. I will give you everything or nothing,
Whichever you need. Your bed is freshly made with striped sheets;
Spaghetti sauce and pies are in the freezer.
I love you. I have kept the feet in perfect condition.

HOW TO ORDER A FREAK:

Neatly. Precisely. Survey its hump.
Chart its topography. Fathom its veined secrets. See
Following pages for our complete spine of hunchbacks.

Sternly. Boat women require discipline.
They are foul-mouthed and the rooster figureheads
Between their breasts crow doubling curses.
See following pages for our complete list
Of canoe babies, frigate girls and steamship women.

Persuasively. Obsequiously. Dwarfs and midgets,
Some say, top the hierarchy. Our inflatable
Model soars higher than ever. Royal colors:
Scarlet and purple, some ermine-trimmed.
Details on following pages.

Look up. Giants loom. In the warp of their arms
The biggest of us can cradle. See following pages
For a complete line of mothers and fathers.

Carefully. Choose one suited to the task:
The betrayed woman to serve you blowfish
On her platter; the tattooed man to print love on
Your skin; the dog-faced boy
To bring you back to God (see Freak holidays)
And the Thin Man with Spare Muscles, the Murmurmaid,
The Guitar Woman, the Electric Bed and many more.
Each one of a kind, so don't delay.

For our complete catalogue,
Send a description of your house
And a full-length photograph of yourself.
Decision of the judges will be final.

THE KILGORE RANGERETTE WHOSE
LIFE WAS RUINED

There we were that beautiful line, synchronized as
A row of pistons in an Eldorado, except
There are only eight of them and there were a hundred of us
(Flowers weeded out of flowers, the cream of the crop).
There we were in the Cotton Bowl, the world-famous
Kilgore Rangerettes, kicking to "The Eyes of Texas Are Upon You"
And they were. In our white cowhide skirts and white felt hats
And red satin shirts and vests with silver stars and
I kicked with the wrong leg and the heel of
My white patent boot got caught in Marybelle's heel on the right
And we both fell and knocked into
The girls on either side of us who sprawled into
Others and half the line went down
Like a keyboard in a demo derby whacked by an axe.

Maybe I should have known—there had been
Problems of appearances before:

Hugging Grandma too tight after she'd had her surgery.
She held the empty place and cried.
Grandpa said she loves you; be more careful.
He bought me a grey suede bag to keep things in.

Giggling in my Hark the Herald Angels Sing duet,
Infecting my partner, too.
The principal said we ruined the Christmas Concert.
My father gave me a garnet and emerald
Synthastone pin in the shape of a clef.

Having a nosebleed when I was shaking hands with
The head of Pan American who came for dinner.
A drop fell on his tan pants.
My father didn't get promoted
But he said that wasn't why.
My mother gave me a box of linen handkerchiefs
Embroidered Monday, Tuesday, Wednesday . . .

Not only did I have to leave the Rangerettes
I left Kilgore, too, even though my roommate,
Who'd been the Maid of Cotton, told me she still loved me.
My intended said the same and gave me
A satin slip, but I don't know . . .
I felt he shouldn't have a ruined wife.
It was that way with any good job, too.
How could I work in the fine crystal section at Neiman's?
All those long-stemmed goblets. Cascades of glass chimes
Woke me every night. I asked to be transferred to
Sterling and Gems. But the tines, the blades, the facets
Menaced me. I learned you break or are broken.
And then a Texaco receptionist, Jack-In-The-Box waitress . . .
No need to spell the perils out.

They know me in Dallas—the only bag lady—lots in NYC—
But all of them are old and I am not. I saw them
On a Kilgore trip to catch the Rockettes and the Balanchine
Swan Lake. (We all agreed those swans would be
Hissed off the field at any Southwest half-time show.)
It's not a bad life. No one expects grace or precision.
Outdoors scavenging the city's trash—presents for yourself—
You collect what you can, what you want, what you need.
Last night I found a Lilly Daché hat and three foam mats.
Street life has its dangers: cold, jail, insults.

But no humiliation. A year ago I got knocked up.
Rape, yes, but no mutilation.
It wasn't bad. I don't feel much these days.
I keep the baby, Billielou, in my bag, snug
In a nest of rags, a Dallas kangaroo.
If Beebeelou—that's what I call her—wants
To be a Rangerette . . . Well, I don't know . . .
Her fingers curl around my thumb like little tongues.
She'll have to have her chance to kick her boots to the sky,
To slice it with her legs, the perfect blue
Deep in the heart of Texas.

NEWS OF THE DEATH OF THE WORLD'S BIGGEST MAN

Today I saw it: Ed Carmel died
And I became the world's biggest man. O, the years I have waited . . .
Ever since . . . it must have been when I was ten and he was twelve
    That I first heard of him.
There was a piece in the Oswego News about a Brooklyn boy who was a little
Over seven feet and weighed three hundred pounds. That's when the rivalry
    Began, at least for me. I do not know
Exactly when he heard of the Wisconsin Peak, as I am known.
Our family name, you see, is Peak. A noble name and one which lent
    Itself to sloganeering in the days
When I was on the road: Peek at Peak, the Mammoth Freak.
Ed, too, was on the road, but not in tents. He had a Rock group:
    Frankenstein and the Brain Surgeons, a catchy name.
One time in Tuscaloosa I saw that he was playing and called him up
And asked if he would like to meet for dinner, but he said
    The truck he used to haul himself around
Had broken down and so he couldn't make it. Some other time, he said.
I really would have liked to see him, to have known how it would feel
    To be smaller than someone. And yet
Today I celebrate. I am the biggest now in the whole world.
I never made nine feet as he did; I stopped at eight foot, ten.
    Never made his weight, either, although
I guess I could have, but I feel better just about four-twenty-five,
Give or take thirty pounds or two plus stone. I like the English way
    Of saying stones, the sense of being
Made of boulders. His obit says his grandfather, at seven feet, was called
The tallest rabbi in the world. Well, mine was called the tallest butcher
    In Wisconsin. When I heard the news that Ed was dead
I felt a rush of loneliness and then of joy. If you must be big

Then biggest is the best. Or so I used to think. That if
        I were the first, the biggest
Then I would be there, would have arrived, but now . . . I think I'll call
Kentucky Fried and say send over a barrel of the Colonel's best
        For the world's biggest man.

IV   A PERFECT BINDING

INVENTORY

I carry a suitcase everywhere with me—and I mean everywhere.
It weighs between nineteen and eighty pounds depending
What I put inside.

> A down-filled pillow, a gray Army
> blanket, a package of Droste bitter
> orange chocolate, my tape recorder
> with a tape of *Der Freischütz*, boots,
> sea-water from Vancouver Bay, next
> rooms opened by Nemerov, Lotte Lehmann's
> "Ich" and my Grandmother's trunk.

The case is useful, but that doesn't justify it; I can't
Justify it. I can only say I need it
Even if

> A down-filled pillow, a gray Army
> blanket, typewriter and Corrasable
> Bond, a bowl of agates from Saudi
> Arabia, popcorn, *Buddenbrooks*, pieces
> of a red glass DANGER sign on which
> I'd cut my knee when I was five
> and disobeyed and walked on Milton Road,
> three fur hats and my Grandmother's trunk.

It interferes. And it does. For example, yesterday afternoon
I met Gunther. I did not know him well, but liked
What I knew.
He asked me if I wanted to see the Whitney Show; I said yes.
At first he didn't seem to notice the suitcase (though

I knew it

Must be what he remembered best about me). Then he did—
I guess when I began dragging. He offered

To check it

And when I said no, to carry it, but I couldn't let him.
At dinner it prevented me, as it always does when

I sit in

A booth, from getting close to the table and I dribbled Marinara
Sauce over it and down my front. I definitely blame

That case for

Making me look messy. When we got in bed it was the same old story:
Three of us. To spell it out: my case gets between me

And friends, especially

If they are not agile or are easily bruised. He tried, but got
So tired he fell asleep. I felt confined and decided to

Stretch out in the bathtub.

It was cozy there after I'd fixed it up with my down-filled
Pillow and gray Army blanket. I took out *Beowulf* and

Some cordial cherries

And my radio and relaxed, thinking, as I so often had,
How well-prepared I am to make the best of

A bad situation.

> A down-filled pillow, a gray Army
> blanket, a hate note to the editor
> of a certain magazine, my radio,
> an empty cordial cherry box, *Beowulf*,
> a tube of Gunther's cobalt blue,
> my left-handed father's left index
> finger and my Grandmother's trunk.

It's true; it is really true; that *is* the case.

OBJETS D'ART

When I was seventeen, a man in the Dakar Station
Men's Room (I couldn't read the signs) said to me:
You're a real ball cutter. I thought about that
For months and finally decided
He was right. Once I knew that was my thing,
Or whatever we would have said in those days,
I began to perfect my methods. Until then
I had never thought of trophies. Preservation
Was at first a problem: pickling worked
But was a lot of trouble. Freezing
Proved to be the answer. I had to buy
A second freezer just last year; the first
Was filled with rows and rows of
Pink and purple lumps encased in Saran wrap.

I have more subjects than I can handle,
But only volunteers. It is an art like hypnosis
Which cannot be imposed on the unwilling victim.
If you desire further information about the process and
The benefits, please drop in any night from nine to twelve.
My place is east of Third on Fifty-sixth.
You'll know it by the three gold ones over the door.

CELEBRATING THE FREAK

The freak is   the other
The freak is   wrapped in lamb cloth because
It is precious
The freak is   precious
The freak is   the other
Alarming us   when it talks through the crook in
                            its arm as it has no mouth

Astounding us   when it threads its legless, armless
                            body through the eye of a needle

Amazing us   when it plays a violin concerto with
                            its feet

The freak wears   well
Though it dies early
The freak wears   silk and velvet to promote its nobility
The freak wears   on the outside what we conceal
The freak wears   down. It becomes tired of being
The freak. It retires   to a country home built to its
Freak specifications: low toilets or moving staircases or
                            beds the size of billiard tables

The freak leaves us   bereft, forcing a little
Mutilation somewhere   to set things right
To wreak   penance
To set   the freak flags flying.

THE STAINED GLASS WOMAN

I

The reason I fall apart easily
Is because they have not discovered
What can hold me together. Lead works
In window junction points, but not in joints.
Other metals are too inflexible. Rubber stretches.
Clay crumbles. Plastics
Are cut by the motion of my glass anxiety.

At the moment I am all in one piece. That is rare.
But then, I am rare. I must acknowledge that:
Glowing, refractive, transparent, colorful.
My mother kept putting pink on top of the other pieces
Until she realized that only made blue, lavender and
Yellow, orange.

Glowing, refractive, transparent, colorful;
Also unbending, fragile and sharp.
"She has a cutting wit," they say.
And I reply, "To wit, to woo; cuckoo, cuckoo,"
Trying to make light, as a stained glass woman should.

II

You knew how to do it, or, rather, did it without completely
Knowing how: made the heart beat, turning blood from blue
To red; made the sections fuse, annealing them; made glass
Into skin. There are no purple or green edges to cut you when

You hold me. Now when I move, I move in unison with myself,
Through places transformed by my transformation.
Only sometimes when the weather changes, or I am tired or angry
Or walk into a church or see a Tiffany lamp, I ache where
The seams once were. Then I am afraid that if you leave me,
A glassy residue may spread through me as quickly
And quietly as the rising light flushes a rose window.

III

You are gone. You were only
The preparation for someone else.
I walk accompanying the prepared space.
My food and furniture are glass.
I look at a glass landscape
And hear glass music.
I protect myself
With the material of myself.
That woman with blood
Reddening the water in the tub
Is the one who can be cut.
I will carry glass flowers to her grave.

APARTMENTS ON FIRST AVENUE

Cemeteries are becoming so crowded in the New York area that a conglomerate has filed plans to construct a block-square above-ground facility.

WNYC News broadcast

Underground space, like water, is running out
So they are building apartment houses for the dead.
That ad: "Keep your loved ones safe from seepage," is
Obsolete; these marble skyscrapers have
No cracks and point in the right direction.
Here, where the municipal station tolls the hour with
"This is New York where more than eight million people
Live and work and enjoy the fruits of democracy,"
The question now becomes where can you afford
To live and where to live and die?

Persephone, her lips stained with pomegranate juice,
Runs in her shift (it is 8 to 4) through the hall.
The seeds from that seedy red globe litter;
They cannot root in marble fields. She plays
Her lyre and the single strand of plaint
Turns polyphonous, echo's counterpoint off
Blue-veined cleavage. Here in the clouds, strains
Of the lyre suffuse the thin air, using it up.
But Zeus, her father, angry at the music of women,
Tells her to go to Hades again even though
The bright stamens of her hair make him want to
Stroke it. She resists his direction. Lightning bolts.
O Lord, the hardness of this place.
She takes the elevator down, abasing herself.

O Lord, the hardness of this place:
Galleries fitted to entomb feeling and bodies,
Sky catacombs where love's declensions stiffen into
Fixity. But I play my lyre and it tells the truth.
Gluck's single strand of happiness resounds.
If you, walking ahead, searching for a bridge to
That most circular of Museums, turn and
Look at me too long, we may both become marble—
Statues for our funerary niche—but we must risk it.
Pluto, Zeus, our parents, the archangel Michael,
The mayor: to Hell with them. Or not.
You reach out your hand and turn. Pulses deny marble.
The ignited fires have no lick of burning.
Defying the Storm King Power Co., we walk out into
The light fantastic, trip the sidewalks. Within our
Bodies' compass no need to fight gravity.

THE LOBSTER

This lobster flown in from Maine to Houston
Lies in a wooden box on cracked ice,
Its green not the green of deep water,
But of decay. Its stalk eyes, which should be
Grains of black caviar, are beads of phlegm.
Through the cracks in its shell, the meat
Shines like oil on water or mother-of-pearl.

I see exactly what it is, yet must wrap it up
In my finest linen handkerchief—the one with
The border and initials pulled by Filipino nuns—
And take it home to keep in my bureau drawer;
So that its smell invades my private places,
And lobster mold begins to form on the edges of fabrics.

I throw open the doors and jalousies, hoping to
Dilute the crustacean air, and you walk in. I had not
Expected to see you again: we had decided.
We inventory everything and redecide: you will stay.
The lobster, smooth and green as deep water, is
Crawling over the blue silk scarf when we
Open the drawer. We cook it for dinner,
In water laved with peppercorns and fennel, and spread
A sheet on the table, anticipating the complete repast.

LETTER TO RICHARD FROM BUDAPEST

I so enjoyed yours from Beyoglu,
It was a feast: Thanksgiving.
Scimitars carved chunks of sky into
Nocturne portions for you and S. Dressing
And undressing. "Our trip," although we both have stumbled
Several times. The course has changed, nearer dessert,
But don't you find it *does* get sweeter?
If this were Beyoglu—Turkish delight?

But this is Hungary. Here M. and I live in Buda,
Looking at Pest across the river. Ginsberg
Came through last month and proclaimed himself the former,
But all the poets here agree that, sitting on a chair atop
A table, instructing them on instant meditation, he was
The latter. The Danube's winter corrugations divide the city.
No ice. But grey. The sky since I arrived grey suede,
Lining an expensive hat. Swatches of the past are here
And we are swathed in them and covered by them,
Or it, the hat. We live beneath that dome of velvet skin,
Brim stitched to the ground. But we as outsiders
Can only guess, a phantom pain, how tight the stitches are.
I do know though, the spires of Szent Istvan Bazilika
Or Parliament's sharp spikes do not pierce through to clearer air;
And the notes of the pervasive gypsy music arc up,
Fall back, spent arrows like the large meandering snow flakes
Intricate as the windows of Matyas Church.
Mary said, "Bring back some pictures of churches which show
Turkish influence." But though the sky is pocked with onions,

Which I believe are Byzantine, I find I do not know
The Moorish from the Magyar. I see you sighing at my ignorance,
One eyebrow lifted as if you'd spotted a misspelling.

Subways here were built before the ones in NYC. They move as if
On air, cost one forint (14¢), and the entrances
Are open, no turnstiles. But last night I put a forint in
And bear-trap jaws sprang closed in front of me; so difficult,
A foreigner and dumb, to find out when and why they close or don't.
Red stars on top of all official buildings.
Here they would carve Turkey with a sickle
Though they detest all their successive conquerors,
The Russians and the Austrians, as well as Turks.
Last week we went to Wien to see *Der Rosenkavalier*, the trip
M's birthday present. Coffee in the dining car,
A perfect measure of Hungary's position:
Not thick as Turkish, nor thin and strong as Viennese,
But gritty black as coal that heated the compartments.
We sipped. A soldier, hands on hips—quite near his gun—
Moved through, clearing the car before him as the border neared,
Reminder that this boarding house is state-controlled.
We come and go, we foreigners. But those who pension here
Can only cross this line every three years.
And not unless their red stars wink in even rows
As our gold ones did in grammar school.

Breakfast at the Pension Zipser was mocha and sweet crescent rolls.
Their shape a badge of honor for the bakers of Vienna,
A patent given them by Ferdinand the First, in 1683 because
They heard, through their bake-oven walls, the tapping of
Invading Turks who tried to break the city by tunneling
Through the ramparts. At first it seemed the rats

Were hungrier than usual, but soon the bakers
Knew and rang the bells and saved Vienna.

At night the neon stars hover over all and join
The crosses here in Budapest to form a black sky tic-tac-toe.
Knock, knock.
Who's there?
A game I think they do not play here
Where knocks at doors evoke too much.
Red star at night; sailors' delight.
Coal barges on the Danube. But we are of the land.
Ours. And though we love the fiery Paprikas, the Poets' Park
On Margarethe Island and Bartók at the Opera,
The twilight of home does gleam whatever
The slubs in its fabric. A protester at home
Here sees the flag's white stars and field of blue and
Hums our anthem. Tonight we go to *Traviata* in Hungarian;
They started that in 1906 to protest King Franz Josef's edict:
"The word of command may *not* be given in Hungarian." Not only
Did the operas switch, but no recruits enlisted that whole year.

The layers here are not like Dobosh torte, each visible,
More like the Danube on a quiet day:
Each transparent, together opaque as oil.
Red star at night; sailors' delight.
Red star in the morning . . . forgive what may be jingoism.

Love flourishes amidst the fiddlers and the cembalos and,
Yes, amidst the stars. I hope it does for you as well, dear
Richard. Red stars in the grey sky. A galaxy parading.
I will be home in March.

BY THE SEA

This is the day of the night it began to turn,
Like milk, slightly sour, still
So close to freshness one is not sure if
The tongue or the cream is at fault.

He, floundering back toward the bay
Like a suddenly beached fish, cannot see that
The water has changed, as if the dairy plant
Behind him had confused its flows, releasing
All its curds the way defective plants can.

He, lunging toward water, does not know,
Has never had to, that even with the ocean's
Grand dilution the balance of fluids has been
Slightly altered, like the shift of residue in
The ear's circular canals. I, experienced
In acute pain, too full of acuity, know
But do not know why milk
Spoils when it seems fresh.

"Your family has had bad luck," he said last night
Just before he found the clocks had stopped
And indicted the house again. Perhaps that is it.
The stroke of his hand makes time seamless but
The clock strikes, even if unheard, and blood poisoning
(Which killed my father's mother when she used
A knitting needle on the fetus, which killed
My uncle when, even with an open cut, he wore
Blue socks) moves through me into him as we come together.

Louis Pasteur, I beg you, seal us in a bottle,
Let us remain bacilli free, save us from relative
Poisons and deaths, from what may prey on us.

It takes awhile to read the ocean,
To see that the prayer is the agent of
What is prayed against. But we've caught it
Early. Let's stop stamping, like spoiled children,
Trying to seal the bargain. Instead
Let's clap our flippers (how I admire
The silvery gloss of sun on your body), spin
Bottles on our noses, beg for
Kippers, and kiss by the beautiful sea.

Until the middle of the twentieth century, book bindings were sewn together before the adhesion of an outer skin of leather or cloth. Since that time, more and more have been glued, a process known as "perfect binding."

Grossbard's Encyclopedia of Bookbinding

A PERFECT BINDING

Glued rather than sewn. The book cracks in
Parts, falls—paper Niagaras of disrepair.
Its separations come at the most used junctions:
Honeymoons, circular hives where arguments wax and
Wane, where cross words escalate; mechanical stairs
Where the Savior escapes his relatives and mounts Heaven;
The mare, saddled in the house where the Madam mother
Reigns in salty splendor.

These places, read and reread, cause the book
To open to those crucial pages, those we must
Touch, tongue to sore spot on the gum: how he
Loves her, how she loves him, how, like Mohawks
Come West to salvage what they could, to survive
Slaughter, they must live on reservations.
No matter what the ceremonies, death is no longer
Responsible for parting the sheets.
Falling apart is laid to resin, mucilage,
Thick as sex.

What kind of thread or twine, what consummate
Glue or paste can bind a man who cannot bear
To have the crotch of his book touched?
He isolates each volume, shelves it, then, with

Passionate indecision, books a partner, holding
The body, ruffling the pages lightly to assure
No fingerprint or line of fold. Reading and
Rereading, he is riveted, then riven.
Distraught: those unstitched avowals, that
Perfect binding.

THE DANGERS OF LOOKING BACK

Men and women could not share the same table and many foods were forbidden to the women and common people under penalty of death.
Ancient Hawaii: The Volcano Museum

The volcano has snow on top, concealing
What is beneath
                  Festooned Stalactite of Basalt
Its shield. We drive toward it through
Forests of tree fern.
                  Bearded Stalactite
Volcano Report (dial 543–2121): This week
Little activity; zero chance of quake.
                  Mass of Driblet
Both men my mother married liked
Their toast burned, would
                  Gas Driblet tube
Send it back to the toaster for blackening:
Charcoal, buttered with preserve.
                  Festooned Paho-e-ho-e
We are walking an arrested lava sea, crunching
Waves under foot: they are black, break
With the sound of burnt toast.
Walking like chewing.
                  Fine-grained Vesicular Basalt
In the hotel, Volcano House, after a meal of
Pork with guavas, slathered rice, Asahi Beer
We go to bed and try to lick

                    Dendritic Aa
The butter off each other until the eruption:
Fountains of fire, red, gold, spurt
                        Gypsum needles
Into the air. We run outside, still naked.
Hot ash flakes down like snow
                    Pele's hair
And a river of orange lava flows toward us like
Movies of a steel mill. When the lava
Coats us
                    Mud raindrops
We are reaching out to each other, not quite
Touching, just as before.
                    Epsom Glauber and Alum Salts

THE RIVER HONEY QUEEN BESS

I

In May it drops down fresh from the mountains,
Dashing silver flakes of water like mica in the air.
Such abundance foils the stones' and hearts' resistance.
    The five dare not broach their wish to dance with water.
    This is the season of their odes.

Early July and not much rain. The pulse slows. Rocks still
Force froth, but the rush is spent. Puckering white
At the selvedge, its weave of blue and green unfurls.
    Three men, two women are rapt in it.
    This is the season of their proposals.

August, and what has always been at the bottom is seen:
Tires, shoes, water moccasins, coral snakes
Braiding in the mud; and what is culturing in
The mirror plates now glazed false blue?
    "A pox on rivers; we always knew," they say.
    This is the season of their attempted escapes.

After the swellings and fevers abate,
The suitors drape themselves in velvet blue and green
To conceal August scars, and order spring-bottled water,
Hoping glass will contain the uncontrollable.
Before they can begin to drink, a swarm escapes—
Gold-dazzle, noise, honey, sting—a circle
Around each head, a crown of May bees.

Truth has been concealed, like 15th-century meat
Rotting under its fabric of spices. Seasons
Have their progression and this is misleading:
The fool's gold suitors believe if May had lasted
They would have found their beloved. Four leave,
Mourning the march of months, the thwarting procession.
But Will stays, through winter's seeming stasis
When blood becomes manageable, to have the Honey Queen again.

This year, no one knows why—a record snowfall? the drift of
Lava ash over the sun? fatigue, sheer as
The cliff beside the river?—June does not begin
On its appointed date. He has not only the month
But its extension to try to pull the river's winding sheet
Through his gold ring, the wedding band which
Plays *The Water Music*. But though he cannot handle
The river which refuses to be treated like
A scarf, he finds he knows her.

August discoveries are not the fault of August. Under
The river's cloak, under the course of its blue blood
Is a slut, a gutter of water and men. The thirst of love
Is slaked by cloacal knowledge. What should Will do?
Cross himself or the river? What can he afford?

He goes to Raleigh to buy the river valley, to build
The Mother Goose Enchanted Village. No more brooding.
Between "The Queen Is in the Parlour Eating Bread and
Honey Golden Manse" and "The Jack Fell Down
and Broke His Crown Hill," the water wends. Will has it
Paved with silver glass, assuring safe reflection; he bends
To face himself. Through flowered banks the mirrored river curves;
Underneath, Honey Queen Bess sings her sting-green music.

A tree, very often an oak (which was a sacred tree) was split in two, the lower part hollowed out like a trough to hold the corpse, the upper part served as a cover.

He brought me a present: a wooden Indian hollowed out
Like a body, hinged in halves. It was painted the colors
Of sea shallows on a bright day, a persimmon, coal,
A chameleon on moss. It was lined in the underfur of seal.
When the wind leaked through the cracks of my house,
Chilling the rooms until they sweated and the rims
Of the rocking chair froze to the floor, I'd close
Myself inside: the Indian would hold onto me.

This special form has been explained by two ancient beliefs: 1) Men were supposed to have grown out of trees.

He took it back, put it in his truck, saying, "I wish
I could let you keep it." I tried to use what I had learned,
Tried to say he needed his own present, but when the cold
Cracked the pitcher on my table and splinters of milk
Patterned the cloth, I drove to his house and, in the dark,
Painted on his door: INDIAN GIVER. I stand behind that.

2) The "tree of the dead" is very much like a dugout, and it may therefore have been considered appropriate for the last journey "across the water." The newly dead were believed to be in an intermediate state between life and death, still possessing a certain awareness of what happened to their bodies.

So when he nears the door, he will hear me
Breathe. When he puts his hand on the knob, he will
Feel my pulse. And he will know me in the warp of his house.

WHY PENELOPE WAS HAPPY

Taking the carrots away from the slave who is peeling them,
Penelope slices, seeing
Wild asses in the woods, woods green and tender as spring lettuce,
Woods dappled silver as the talents of men gambling in market sun.
Ulysses is in that wood.
She knows it; seers recognize their visions as distinct from other seeing.
Tears run down her cheeks and
Seep through her rosy fingers onto the carrots.
She hands the splayed bunch back to the slave, saving only one.

To her dawn room, the place where light first pries
Its illumination through the columns, to her loom, one of many woven
Through the palace like the alabaster urns, urns full of
Dark wine to remind them of the sea.
Seated, she replaces her olive wood shuttle with the carrot,
"Show me again where he is." Yellow threads ravel
From it, like hair, to become sun on the forest floor.
Ulysses stands, a boar's bladder
To his lips, wine trickling through his beard,
Streaking its silver threads red.
She weeps with happiness. He is safe and
Far.
"Daphne watch over him," she prays, weaving leaves of laurel.

To be alone in your domain—
A queen within, a king without and distant—
Such stately pleasure, such companied solitude.
Now he and his men are boarding the barque, herding the wild asses
Who bray with fear before them. Now they are setting sail.
Now they are safely at bay.

The barque's cheek paint reflects its unwinking eye in the water's glaze,
Soothing the Gods. Her unpainted cheek flares
As late morning light
Pries its way through the columns
To touch her, a sign
It is time to move to the noon room where she will work on Apollo,
Burning her fingers as she caresses the golden threads of his hair.

There is a certain chill so deep inside it will not yield
To layers of down or wires telegraphing warmth through wool—
Another quilt upon the mound—no comforts can amend it.
Passion's enactments—flaring, flaming—trumpet heat and melt
The flesh yet—like a stone-graved alphabet—the granite cold
Is there incised and sharp. Even anger's once sure fire
Burns with ice flamed dry. Long lines—extended like a wartime
Queue for meat—accrue no remedy; extension is
A form of prolongation—the poet's cure—but what will be
Prolonged cannot be willed. Nothing is impossible
To understand: one times nought is nought, which leaves one clear
Of lover's rubble. And warm as love conceived in logic's sphere.
When heat resists all stratagems, escape to greater cold,
The wrap of arctic circuses—go North to vault the Pole.

THOSE WHO LIVE ALONE

When good news comes, wonder why, though they have been
Waiting and waiting for the kettle to work itself into a fury,
Releasing celebratory plumes of steam into the cool air,
Though they have been watching and watching—and the boil
Is so lancingly slow—why then does the actual moment
Lack all lustre? The mind encompasses the message and signals
This is now a time of happiness. Neurons do their work,
Synapses join or snap to attention, whatever they do, all parts
Of the body acknowledge receipt. There is even
A certain amount of action: calls to those who will be pleased,
From those whose voices are feathery with congratulation.
The kettle whistles on in an explosion of vapours
Which should make the one who lives alone faint with joy.

Instead the air fills with damp, foreshadowing twinges
Of loss and other infirmity so at home it settles down as if
To stay. In pleating litanies of inattention, the lacks
Crease themselves more and more sharply into edges until they form
A paper fan which lies beside the blue cup full of amber tea.
Blue cup on green table with white fan. And the one who lives alone,
Admiring the fan, the style of its making, the knife-edge of
Its folds, the precision of its dilemmas, snaps it open and shut,
Open and shut, looking away from the door, the blue door,
Looking away, no longer willing to invite the actual.

V ALTERNATE MEANS OF TRANSPORT

A SEQUENCE

... The modern study of chaos began with a creeping realization in the 1960's that quite simple mathematical equations produced results every bit as violent as a waterfall. Tiny differences in input could quickly become overwhelming differences in output—a phenomenon given the name "sensitive dependence on initial conditions." In weather, for example, this translates into what is only half-jokingly known as the Butterfly Effect—the notion that a butterfly flapping its wings today in Peking might affect the weather next month in New York.
James Gleick, "Solving the Mathematical Riddle of Chaos"

On August summer nights, a panama hat may be conceived as a halo.
Howard Moss

I THE LAWN: NEW DESIGNS

Hats blow away, sailing, swirling over
The bright green lawn—mostly straws: boaters, panamas,
The pale, large-brimmed ladies' versions, sailors,
Streamers and ribands fluttering like kite tails,
Leghorns of Tuscan wheaten straw, its color clear,
Delicate and golden, crenelated towers of Irish thicket straw,
A few cloches for those who like to wear
Their halos pulled down over their ears.

But also, silk hats, buckram-bodied, patterned with
A plush of brilliant gloss or varnish-stiffened calico,
Wimples, tops, velvet mob caps like heavy breasts, cocked
Of straw and felt, lace milking tams, one Flaundrish beaver.
And the panoply of people chasing, twirling,
Tripping, jumping. Ballet after Bournonville on the green.
Painting after Brueghel, repainted Chagall, on the green.

Everyone but the man with a butterfly net is laughing
Or smiling; such amiable pursuits.
Some of the high-flyers are swathed in veils—
Victorian clouds—or spangled mantillas where the sun
Strikes a patch of mist. The commotion, synchronized as
The word tells us, amazing in such a small space,
That verdant lawn on the head of a pin. For of course they,
Like us, are minuscule and lose their heads even more easily.
They will continue their *Hosanna*s and *Salva Me*s
No matter what. No matter . . . or so some say.

The man with the butterfly net, enthralled by quarrels of
Glass but not of words, inspects the action of
A Spangled Fritillary's wings, which might yield a new model
For the community. He envisions the firmament suffused
With orange and black as the Host descends wearing his creation.
A flutter of descent, yes, orange and black, as if snow
Had taken on the colors of All Hallow's Eve,
Leaving the sanctity of white for something less determinate.
The Spangled Fritillary alights on a lilac's flowery fist.
The net fills with air, as if it were a capuchin, and
Rings the branch enveloping its prey.

The Curator lectures on "The Triptych of Heaven and Hell" by
Capelli, "See the border friezes of angels repeating
The lower motifs of clustering stars." He is using
His pointer of light to pick out details of the work;
Circles of light halo this figure or that, giving it
The strange magnification of tight focus.
"See the Jew skating, the man in his nightclothes
Chasing the visibles with his butterfly net, see the organist.
And there I am in the left-hand corner of the center panel;
See the circle of my light ringing the blue and white saucer
From which the cat is licking cream thick as paint.
The painter, too, is there: yes, the man with the net,
But also the prisoner, the acolyte, the lover stroking
The buttocks of his love whose leghorn, trimmed with
Daisies and red ribands, lies beside her on the grass,
The woman carrying a boil pot and a protest banner.
Look further: how many other places can you locate the painter?"
A sudden wind blows through the gallery where they stand
Listening to the lecture. The lighter hats threaten to lift,
Tugging at the hairpins of some of the bystanders,
But the touch of a hand is enough to subdue them.

3 THE SKATING RINK

The bearded Jew skates differently as he practices
His curls, addressing the ice with rabbinical argument.

A certain stiff grace in the arms and thin chest, a wiggle
In the hips as if something out of Salome remains embedded there.

He stands out on ice embroidered by everyone else twirling
(Whirling), gliding (sliding), checking

(Pecking with the beaks of their skates). He knows he is
Distinct from all the others and wonders again, why?

His solemnity? No; the oriental girl repeating eights is equally;
So is the boy practicing hockey moves, goals, the hat trick.

And the whole beginners' class flapping
Across the ice like newborn chicks.

Is it because of what he writes with the blades of his skates,
Determined to keep the words of the Torah alive

By inscribing them on ice? He knows that he has never
Been able to answer, has been forced to accept

A strange combination of fear and pride which he cannot
Lose, cannot outrace, does not wish to outrace.

In mirrors at the side of the rink he sees the halo
His hair makes around his yarmulke and around the hair

A circle of white moths like the rings of Jupiter,
Like flakes of light, like the swirl of snow around

An empty bird's nest, and wonders if he forgot
To put camphor in the woolens last spring.

4   THE ROLE OF HATS IN ILLNESS

Here we see the water converted by the fire
Into a vapour, which ascends from the pot and meets
The pot's hat whose lower temperature makes it condense
Into drops. It is even so with the human body:

The watery phlegm originates in the southerly region of
The intestines and in disease is heated by
The fire of the liver; it rises again on the third day
To the colder region of the head where it coalesces in
Warm droplets. These are the cause of ear infection,
Sattin coughs, torn veils, moth holes, catarrh and coryza.
The body's mean has tippled so one suffers side effects of
Headache, aesthetic fault and all forms of bonnet vertigo.

5 THE CHURCH

The organist plays the Michaelmas Magnificat,
Each needle of sound a silver spike
Crowning his head. It is his work; as Kappelmeister
He both writes and plays. At his feet, there is
A basin for slops, the debris from the nether region
With its tumescent liver, its coils of lights,
Its laden kidneys, its decomposing spleen.
Delivering music, he picks the basin up and puts it on.
It rests uncomfortably atop the spiked crown, driving
The heavenly deeper into his head as he leaves for bed.

6 THE DEMOCRACY OF HATS

The felts meet in Congress: they cast
Lots, salt, everything to the wind.
And couple.

The peaked caps, engorged with braid, meet
In a dictatorship: they cast
Lots, pillars, statues of the leader, firing
Them in the oven for days.

The straws are the most disorganized: they cast
Lots to see which head they wish to crown
On this glorious summer day
Which is itself impervious
To the body politic.

*And when they have put on cloak, rapier, plumed hat, scarlet-gold-
tissue breeches, etc., they descend to the women and order feasting to
commence. If they follow the wisdom of Avicenna, they will alternate
all the windy meats with a decoction of the condite fruit of wild rose,
parsley roots and centaury until lust issues forth, breeding all that is
copious and universal, those divers truths which divert humors, aches,
winds, etc.*

Oliver Rowland, REMEDIES AGAINST DISCONTENTS

7   BENEFIT BALL FOR SAVE THE CHILDREN

Great scurfs of food are borne in, piled so high they
Drip onto embroidered carpets where lovers, bare of
Hats, lie entwined. The serving men step over them
Lifting roasts and joints, towering jellies shaking their
Church colors, nests of tatted squab and quail, berries
Staining clotted cream, bisques, broths, chowders, thorny
Silhouettes of artichoke and pineapple, pastries and pasties
Oozing drops of kidney juice and bits of beef, and all
The nouns of nourishment too crammed with
Stuff and sauce to make their source discernible.

There is finally enough so that if food be the food of
Love they can play on and in it and, satiated, be carried off
In great scurfs, as if the scales of extinct animals,
The platters on which they sprawl, were music and
The rocking motion came from the wind, not from
The apprehension that, in an agony of indigestion, they
Have turned their hats into pudding basins, into
Breast adornments, into buttock fetish bowls, denying
The struggle that circular shapes insist on if
They are to serve at all. These lovers see the universe as

Self-contained, a metaphor, they state, which has the ring
Of truth. And they twist and turn on their scurfs
Feeling that inside of them, in an agony of indigestion,
The maw of the universe is farting something which
Could not possibly be hats.

8 THE MUSEUM

"Here there are flights of angels like
Small albino flies. See the fine-haired robes,
The glassen wings, the compound eyes. They crowd
The field within the frame. Note the multiplicity
Inside those eyes. The seraphim within, reflected by
The pupils of cherubim. You look confused.

"Actually what you are frowning at is white canvas,
Paint still in the vat, a snow field on which we,
Who understand the many shades of meaning, will paint.
The artist has at hand only the hues of his short span,
The transports of his time. But every century
Critics create afresh the apprehending vision."

The wind asserts its will, sweeping the museum,
The negative wind of fire, sucking,
Giving vent, inhaling the curator, the bystanders,
The painting and the wall on which it hangs,
The museum entire in fiery discontent.

9 THE C MAJOR MASS WITH FLIES

Flies invade the eyes of the people drowsing on
The south lawn. The fly bodies, in their black,
Mother-of-pearl casings, carry eggs to be laid
In the pupil's optic dark. Wings, soldered
Like the leaded glass of Gothic glaziers, fold in
After entry.

Flies in the eyes enact the flying that is in
Each of them, all goggle and sequin virtuosity—
World War I aces—all act and axe—hatchet murderers
On the moor. The liquid drowse of noon is stopped
By the agony of penetration, itch, encrustation
As flies mate and leave the eye's incubator
To circle around heads; halos of flies,
Crowns of flies, shimmering, musical, open to
Interpretation.

The people on the dry, smooth-shaven lawn begin to run,
Circling in steps like those of the generations of
Hat-chasers but they wear no hats, only
Masses of flies in their open buzzing circles;
And the people run to escape reinvasion, smelling

Rank fruit as they wave their arms hoping
To dispel the tarnished silver clouds of vertu
Turned; run and twist, Graham dancers on the green.
And exterminators seed abandoned hats,
Which could be bowls of incubation,
With toxins.

The cycle is beyond human agency;
Flies intent without intention on their performance
Of *Paradise* penetrate deep into the set of
The eye which is painted brighter than
Crimson Lake or Crystal Azure. Flies of
The evening's Mass emerge from the wings,
Work their way forward like ranks of soldiers
Or counter choirs. Even in this time of indecision
Certain agonies induce in the most languid, a need
For solutions: argyrol, silver nitrate, gentian violet.
But ... not yet. Not yet. Only
A glimmer of hope.

The Jewish Talmudists take upon them to determine how God spends His whole time . . . sometimes overseeing the world, etc., like Lucian's Jupiter, that spent much of the year painting butterflies' wings, and seeing who offered sacrifice; telling the hours when it should rain, how much snow should fall in such a place, which way the wind should stand in Greece, which way in Africa.

Robert Burton, THE ANATOMY OF MELANCHOLY

10   THE GLASS-WALLED CONSERVATORY

The man with the butterfly net has given up on wings.
He sits at the drawing board applying the shape of crystals
To the shape of hats: lace, facet, line of fault.
"More applicable to heads," he says, bending over the board,
Drawing essential structures so finely delineated
They rise off the page like the angels they are meant to adorn.

His name begins with *L* or so the others who call him insist—
Leonardo, Lucifer, Li Po. . . . He answers indifferently,
Knowing that in his century cause and effect are blurred
And everything turns back upon itself. The Sistine Chapel ceiling,
As close to heaven as many feel they will come, is most easily
Looked at for long periods of time by holding
A mirror in your hands and looking down.

In the night sky around the Conservatory, hats
Are going past in flames. Hat meteors, hat fire storms
Flash past as L. continues to draw. The heavenly host
Watches its visible badge of sanctity
Decorate the heavens with fiery hoops and loops as if
A circus arena were being set for tygers. The host
Squints as the halos move further out
And settle over spheres to marry—bright, varnished rings
Around the planets of distant galaxies.

Through the balance of terror, we all come to hold a dagger to the hearts of those nearest and dearest to us as well as to threaten those far away . . . The parent threatens the child, the lover the lover, the friend the friend, the citizen the citizen. Our acceptance of nuclear weapons is in that sense a default of parenthood, of love, of friendship, of citizenship . . . And in making a "conscious choice" to lift the nuclear peril . . . we resolve to clear the air of the smell of burning flesh.

Jonathan Schell, THE ABOLITION

11 THE HAT FACTORY

The hat in the hands of the hatmaker catches fire.
She is not surprised; she has always thought one would;
The heat where she works causes inflammation every summer.
Not for nothing did the garment center give birth
To the term sweatshop. Flames lick the brim. Storms
Caused by atmospheric tension break, and the spot
Where the roof has always leaked acts as a fire extinguisher.
"Piss pot," she says, holding the felt in her hands.
Blisters rise on them. The burns are not too bad.
But what about the children alone at home?

With what astonishment he saw the silk dresses with great gauze
wings pinned to their backs by scarab brooches catch fire just as the
band concert began, as if breath from the sounding brasses fanned the
flames. It was a moment when his vision of the redemptive had to be
recovered again, as if history were only an old sofa.

        Placido Santos, STOREHOUSE OF REMARKABLE ATONEMENTS

12   THERE CAME A WIND

Hats fly around the museum as the wind
Grows from zephyr to breeze reversing
The order of things. In moments of
Abatement when it seems *the ominous is past,*
And the universe has stopped breathing,
Hats come to rest

        On the heads of Nefertiti, Aphrodite,
        The Thinker (3rd casting), the Degas ballerina
        In her gauze tutu, on the discus of
        The Discus Thrower, the spear of the knight
        In the Great Hall of Armor, on the penis of
        One of the putti circling King Oswin's bed,
        On the breast hole of a reclining Henry Moore,
        On the cross being readied for Christ,
        On Cleopatra's needle and on and on.

The bystanders chasing their hats
Begin to laugh at the odd adornments;
Even the curator permits himself a smile.
And the wind runs through the fingers of statues
And slides along the frames of paintings,
Making music out of art. And the hats,

Like mutes of trumpets or trombones,
Damp the sound down just enough
So there is no pain for those in the halls and galleries,
Only a dancing exhilaration. And out through
The mouth and eyes of the Museum music spills down the Avenue.

A red hat in a dream may, as Freud told us, be a genital symbol, doff-ing one's hat, as in circumcision or deflowering. Or it could be seen as a form of double reversal; so that red reverses to blue, the celestial, the heavenly and the head (hat) becomes the feet (shoes) moving up-ward toward the kingdom of heaven. A third reading would be that red hat is an anagram for hatred, the sexual self turning against itself.
THE PSYCHOANALYTIC DICTIONARY OF DREAM SYMBOLS

13 A FLOURISH OF CASUAL KILLING

The glass dome of Heaven above the Conservatory
Falls in from the aftershock, cutting the soft parts
Of the night sky to shreds. Black shreds and glass
Imprinted with galaxies and hat nebulae shower down,
Announcing in a flourish of fragments that
The universe is both finite and infinite.

For those alone and makeless there is the carnal pleasure of
Hats, genital amazements as the *bracelet of bright hair*
About the bone is capped: an ocelot toque, a tam-o'-shanter,
Loose slide of Muslim veil, loll of sateen bagnolette,
Anthem tattoo of helmet pot and all,
All only exquisite mimicry of flesh on flesh, as planetarium
Stars, the sky and cats, the cry of babies.

After beatitude, the lonely rise, not with the calm
Swelling of bread but with marsh fever, malarial
In its reliefs and returns. The lonely call for order,
Invoking clerical devices: fasts, strict columns,
A new and secret prison of the pulses, no more loose ends.

Where like a pillow on a bed, a pregnant hat swells up
Its yield will be a relic of desire,
A bronzed bonnet on the bedside table and
The knowledge of those alone: what's done cannot be
Undone; our enmities unite us, not our loves.

I want to paint men and women with that something of the eternal which the halo used to symbolize.

Van Gogh's letters

14 DEPENDING ON THE SALVATION OF HATS

The people are gone.
Only the hats remain (reminding us
Of man's capacity for destruction).
Visible badges of sanctity litter
The spangled heavens long after
What we value them for is extinct,
Reminding us, tugging
At our hems or trousers
Like a child wanting attention,
That the child's hat may be here
Long after the child,
That half-lives of bliss or torment,
Lies of escape routes are
Equally irrelevant and that if
This is true, it is an obvious lie,
Addressed as it must be,
If true, to hats.
We try to keep the underlying truths
Where we can't see them, that boy
In the story with the rich butter,
Cool stream butter, under
The protection of his hat,
Walking, twirling, jumping
In the radiance of the sun.

The problems resulting from defining and describing complex conflicts
by use of simple conflict models are manifold. Almost tautologically,
we can say that as a consequence of this simple modelling, the complex
conflict will be represented in an oversimplified fashion.
Frank Moulaert, "On the Nature and Scope of Complex Conflicts"
PEACE SCIENCE SOCIETY

15   THE DIALECTIC OF THE HATLESS

The curator is fondling tiger's-eye cufflinks,
The Jew is shopping at the Safeway, the man with the net
Is drawing in the Conservatory, the hatmaker is
Reading *Crusaders in the Bosphorus* to her children,
The organist is lying in the stained sheets of his scurf,
Transported by his new cantata, "The Golden Mean,"
The curator is lecturing the painter, who is filing her nails,
"The trouble is, in a time without absolutes,
God's will, the King's, the family's, the tribe's,
No longer crowned with certainty, one understands
How tedious absolute freedom is."
"No. How frightening. Yet, perhaps a form of bliss.
The liquefaction of our hats may force salvation on us," she says.
"I would like to frame these dilemmas for you," he says.
"You always do. I'm returning to the lawn."

The man with the net is drawing in the Conservatory,
Pulling the strings tighter, making sure that
What can be secure is; the organist is staring at
The bronze hat on his bureau, the Jew
And the hatmaker are drinking tea,
"Isn't it only your own death and, possibly,

The destruction of what you, yourself, have made—
Music, books, flower beds—that you can really feel?"
"Only your children," says the hatmaker, giving suck to
The rosy mouth of her youngest. "Also," says the Jew
Who has no children, "your hats."

I have always found that Angels will have the vanity to speak of them-
selves as the only wise; this they do with a confident insolence sprout-
ing from systematic reasoning.

                    Blake, "The Marriage of Heaven and Hell"

16 AT THE ROUND EARTH'S ENDURING CORNERS

If we, all brimless, had the comfort of hats,
Or even if we did not but were sure they, with
Their hats, were standing there all pins and needles
To save us, filling the sky with the snow of
Their muslin boaters, their immaculate certainties,
We could relax into that sureness which the cleavage
Of good into good and evil brings. Instead,
We consult language, a paltry vehicle
For salvation. See how it falters,
Deprived of hats and hosannas.
        No . . . Not yet . . .
Is what we are left with. No epiphany or apotheosis.
The net of glittering firmaments
Now pin-pointed as what it is.
        And yet, perhaps . . . Hush don't raise . . .
        Or is . . . Keep it under your . . .
It is unspeakable.
        Perhaps that is why . . . We may live after . . .
        Perhaps . . .
A quiet ending.

Paradox is not comfortable; its X exposes that; too many
Cross-purposes to allow you to settle exquisitely poised
As a Spangled Fritillary on the lace of a blooming lilac branch,
As the sexless angels on the head of a pin.

O A B C D angels says Leonardo.
M R no angels says the Jew, Y Z what can't be?
The bystanders wring their hands as if they were bells.
Stop playing, they tell the organist and the poet,

And both could, could make a surface
Clear, calm and reflective, a voluptuous skin,
Giving lap and lull, lap and lull. I could
Take you back to the lawn, now studded

With its spring brocade of flowers, to a sky
Studded with hats, to a sky lavish with hats.
Poems lavish with the language of light wing through a time when
We are in the dark. Illuminated by static, by the electricity

Of the synthetic, love—a plain song, a plaint—is asked
To do more than it can. It is, perhaps, what we have left.

POEMS IN THIS VOLUME ARE
DEDICATED AS FOLLOWS:

Vain Remedy—for Gay Block and Malka Drucker

Separations—for Glenn and Kathleen Cambor

Envy of Old Husbands—for Donald Barthelme, who claimed it as his

*And Cause His Countenance To Shine Upon You
—for Barbara Kellerman*

A Critical Age—for Helen Frankenthaler

*At the Round Earth's Imagin'd Corners: A Stack of Marriage Boxes
—for James Surls, though it really was with him*

The Triborough Bridge a Crown for His Head—for Hans Namuth

The Tune He Saw—for James Thompson

The Marschallin Gives a Voice Lesson—for Jonathan Greenwald

The Stained Glass Man—for Donald Hirst

Mother of the Sun—for Judy Collins

The Four Virginias—for Virginia Carmichael

*Celebrating the Freak—for May Swenson, who agreed to the
dedication, understanding what was being celebrated.*

The Stained Glass Woman—for WAC

Apartments on First Avenue—for Howard Moss

Letter to Richard from Budapest—for Richard Howard

A Perfect Binding—for Myron Simon

The River Honey Queen Bess—for Lucia Greer

Why Penelope was Happy—for Eve France

Alternate Means of Transport—for Robert Gilliland

Cynthia Macdonald was born in New York City, and received her B.A. from Bennington College and her M.A. from Sarah Lawrence College. She has taught at Sarah Lawrence and Johns Hopkins University and is now a professor at the University of Houston, where she founded the creative writing program in 1979. Since 1972, she has published five collections of poems, *Amputations, Transplants, (W)holes, Alternate Means of Transport* and the present volume. Her grants and awards include a National Endowment for the Arts grant, a Guggenheim Fellowship, and a National Academy and Institute of Arts and Letters Award in recognition of her achievement in poetry. Formerly an opera singer, Cynthia Macdonald has written two opera librettos. She is a graduate of the Houston-Galveston Psychoanalytic Institute, and an academic member of the American Psychoanalytic Association.

A NOTE ON THE TYPE

This book was set on the Linotype in Granjon, a type named after
Robert Granjon. George W. Jones based his designs for this type
upon that used by Claude Garamond (c. 1480–1561) in his beautiful French books. Granjon more closely resembles Garamond's
own type than do the various modern types that bear his name.
Robert Granjon began his career as type cutter in 1523 and was
one of the first to practice the trade of type founder apart from
that of printer.

Composed by Heritage Printers, Inc., Charlotte, North Carolina
Printed and bound by Halliday Lithographers,
West Hanover, Massachusetts

Typography and binding design based on originals
by Dorothy Schmiderer Baker